Celebrate
THE Century™

A COLLECTION OF
COMMEMORATIVE STAMPS

1920-1929

CELEBRATE 10 THE CENTURY®
PUT YOUR STAMP ON HISTORY
1900 ▪ 2000

UNITED STATES POSTAL SERVICE®

UNITED STATES POSTAL SERVICE

POSTMASTER GENERAL
AND CHIEF EXECUTIVE OFFICER
Marvin Runyon

CHIEF MARKETING OFFICER AND
SENIOR VICE PRESIDENT
Allen Kane

EXECUTIVE DIRECTOR, STAMP SERVICES
Azeezaly S. Jaffer

MANAGER, STAMP MARKETING
Valoree Vargo

PROJECT MANAGER
Gary A. Thuro Jr.

TIME LIFE BOOKS

TIME-LIFE BOOKS IS A DIVISION OF TIME LIFE INC.

TIME-LIFE BOOKS

PRESIDENT
Stephen R. Frary

TIME-LIFE CUSTOM PUBLISHING

VICE PRESIDENT AND PUBLISHER
Terry Newell

VICE PRESIDENT OF
NEW BUSINESS DEVELOPMENT
Michael A. Hurley

DIRECTOR OF NEW PRODUCT DEVELOPMENT
Teresa Graham

EDITORIAL STAFF FOR CELEBRATE THE CENTURY

MANAGING EDITOR
Morin Bishop

EDITORS
Sally Guard, John Bolster

DESIGNERS
Barbara Chilenskas, Jia Baek

WRITERS
Merrell Noden, Eve Peterson

RESEARCHERS
*Jenny Douglas,
Jessica Goldstein, Lauren Cardonsky*

PHOTO EDITOR
Bill Broyles

First printing. Printed in U.S.A.

TIME-LIFE is a trademark of Time Warner Inc. U.S.A.

LIBRARY OF CONGRESS CATALOGING-IN-PUBLICATION DATA
Celebrate the century: a collection of commemorative stamps.
p. cm. Includes index.
Contents: v. 3. 1920–1929
ISBN 0-7835-5319-6
1. Commemorative postage stamps—United States—History—20th century.
2. United States—History—20th century.
I. Time-Life Books

HE6185.U5C45 1998
769.56973—DC21

97–46952
CIP

Books produced by Time-Life Custom Publishing are available at a special bulk discount for promotional and premium use. Custom adaptations can also be created to meet your specific marketing goals. Call 1-800-323-5255.

PICTURE CREDITS

Contents

Introduction
4

PROHIBITION
10

MARGARET MEAD
16

BABE RUTH
22

THE GATSBY STYLE
28

EARLY RADIO
34

ART DECO STYLE
40

JAZZ EXPLOSION
46

EMILY POST'S *ETIQUETTE*
52

EDWARD HOPPER
56

THE FOUR HORSEMEN
62

FLAPPERS
68

CHARLES LINDBERGH
74

THE 19TH AMENDMENT
80

ELECTRIC TOY TRAINS
86

THE STOCK MARKET CRASH
90

Index
96

The '20s were a decade of towering cultural icons such as Ruth (left) and Lindbergh (above).

INTRODUCTION

"It was an age of miracles, it was an age of art, it was an age of excess, and it was an age of satire," wrote F. Scott Fitzgerald in 1931, as he looked back on the giddy, delirious years between the end of the Great War in 1918 and the stock market crash of 1929. These were the Roaring Twenties, the Jazz Age, one of the rare times in American history when something approximating a cultural revolution took place. Americans—wealthy Americans at least—threw off their dark cloak of puritanism and celebrated the end of the war and the arrival of prosperity with a desperate gaiety.

It was an age of tremendous recklessness too, on Main Street and especially on Wall Street, and home run slugger Babe Ruth, a barrel-chested, seemingly omnivorous man with a nickname that reflected the era's infatuation with youth, was the perfect hero for it. "I swing big, with everything I've got. I hit big or I miss big," said Ruth. "I like to live as big as I can."

A nation hellbent on celebration had room for other heroes, too. This was the era of Charles Lindbergh and Red Grange; of Louis Armstrong and Duke Ellington; of jazz and illicit booze and flappers and the Charleston, and of dance marathons and flagpole sitting. Playing analyst to a generation, Fitzgerald wrote, "Something had to be done with all the nervous energy stored up and unexpended in the War."

At the beginning of the decade, scholarly, reserved Woodrow Wilson was still president. Wilson had persuaded the country to enter World War I by advertising it as a "war to end all wars" and a "war to make the world safe for democracy." He had hoped to leave the League of Nations as his greatest legacy. But for Americans the Great War had been anything but a triumphant experience.

It was in many ways the first modern war, and it had horrified soldiers and civilians alike with its trenches and planes and poison gas—the ugly technology of mass slaughter. One popular story told of a soldier who, returning from Europe, sailed into New York Harbor and called out to the Statue of Liberty, "Lady, once I get behind you, I promise I never will look at your face again."

The United States was unquestionably the most powerful nation on earth in 1920, but Americans wanted no part of policing the rest of the world. Sensing the mood of the country, Congress cut the army from 288,000 men to 175,000 the following year.

The presidential election of 1920 pitted Republican Warren G. Harding, a U.S. senator from Ohio and publisher of the *Marion Star*, against Ohio governor James M. Cox, a Democrat whose background was also in small-town journalism. Cox's first act as nominee was to travel to Washington to pay homage to Wilson. But by embracing the incumbent, Cox also embraced Wilson's unpopular policies and virtually guaranteed his own defeat. Harding, whose campaign included a pledge to "return to normalcy," won roughly 60 percent of the popular vote.

As they were turning their backs on the world, some Americans were also coming to resent the non-Americans in their midst. The '20s began with the arrest of Nicola Sacco and Bartolomeo Vanzetti, Italian immigrants charged with murdering two shoe factory employees in South Braintree, Massa-

Armstrong was perhaps jazz's most effective evangelist.

chusetts. Though the evidence was entirely circumstantial and Sacco had a rock solid alibi—he had been visiting the Italian consulate in Boston when the crime was committed—those weaknesses in the state's case gave way before the supposedly damning facts that both were immigrants and, even worse, anarchists. Sacco and Vanzetti were found guilty and sentenced to execution, which was carried out in 1927.

Unsettled by a wave of violent labor disputes, many of which were organized by radical immigrants, and by the continuing aftershocks of the Russian Revolution, Congress passed a series of laws aimed at restricting immigration. First came the Emergency Quota Act of 1921, which limited the total number of immigrants per year to 360,000. The National Origins Act of 1924 lowered that total to 150,000 and specified that 90 percent had to come from northwestern Europe and none from Japan.

The decade was a time of major demographic shifts in the United States, particularly among blacks, whose "Great Migration" from the rural south to the industrial north, which had been a crucial part of girding for war, accelerated. In 1920, when the price of cotton plummeted from $1 to 10 cents a pound, Robert S. Abbott, the publisher of the nation's most influential black newspaper, the *Chicago Defender*, launched what he called "The Great Northern Drive," urging blacks to leave the Mississippi Delta for the greater freedom and economic opportunities available to them in the North. The number of blacks in Chicago, which between 1910 and 1920 had grown from 44,000 to 109,000, would swell again in the '20s, to 234,000.

With them came jazz, the syncopated, sensual music that had originated in New Orleans and made its way up the Mississippi River to Memphis, St. Louis and finally Chicago. Cornetist Louis (Satchmo) Armstrong made that very trip in 1922 to join Joe (King) Oliver's Creole Jazz Band, and the following year he made his first recording.

Indeed, 1923 was a watershed year for music as both Bessie Smith and Jelly Roll Morton made their first recordings and Duke Ellington began playing a Harlem club called Barron's Cabaret. Elsewhere in New York City, George Gershwin, who as a boy had ridden his bicycle up to 134th Street to listen to ragtime, was composing a kind of symphonic jazz in works like *Rhapsody in Blue*, which premiered at Aeolian Hall in 1924.

Prohibition resulted in the disposal of massive quantities of liquor.

Not everyone was pleased with these developments. In 1925 Henry Ford organized a national series of folk dances in an attempt to combat what he regarded as the pernicious influence of jazz. Blacks found themselves in serious danger. A race riot in Tulsa in 1921 led to the deaths of 200 people, black and white, and 1,400 members of the revitalized Ku Klux Klan staged a march through New York City.

Mark Twain once wrote that "nothing so needs reforming as other people's habits." Nowhere was that corrective impulse more evident than in the most misguided and ultimately counterproductive piece of legislation in U.S. history. That was, of course, the 18th Amendment to the Constitution, which forbade the sale, manufacture and transportation of alcoholic beverages. Prohibition became the law of the land on January 17, 1920, and remained so until 1933, when it was repealed by the 21st Amendment.

It is impossible to calculate precisely how much damage the temperance forces did in the name of reforming the sinners in their midst. Certainly Prohibition turned many otherwise law-abiding citizens into criminals and generally eroded their respect for the law. In 10 years the federal government made more than 500,000 arrests. Even worse, Prohibition did more to spawn organized crime than any other single force. Here was a huge black market in which crafty or ruthless bootleggers could make a killing—which they quite literally did in many cities. In the St. Valentine's Day Massacre of 1929, seven members of Bugsy Moran's gang were machine-gunned to death by members of Al Capone's gang in a Chicago garage. With the end of Prohibition, the new criminal class simply turned its efficient network to prostitution, gambling and drugs.

For the moneyed classes, the '20s were a time of indulgence. Fitzgerald credited the decade with giving rise to the cocktail party, but the extrava-

In later years, Rockne (center) had several reunions with the legendary Four Horsemen.

gant parties he describes in *The Great Gatsby* show the hollowness beneath the gleaming surface of the age.

With more free time and more spending money than ever before, Americans turned out in record numbers to watch sports events. Before 1919, no one had ever hit more than 24 home runs in a single baseball season. Ruth hit 29 in 1919, then astonished everyone the following year by slugging 54. Still, in the glittering firmament of the '20s, the Golden Age of American Sports, the Bambino was but one star. Vying for headline space with him were heavyweight champ Jack Dempsey; Illinois halfback Red Grange; tennis player Bill Tilden, who won six straight U.S. singles titles from 1920 to 1925; Bobby Jones, who won nine major tournaments in the '20s en route to winning golf's only recognized Grand Slam, in 1930; and Knute Rockne and his Notre Dame football juggernaut, which featured the renowned Four Horsemen for several seasons, and went 105–12–5 in his 13-year tenure as coach, from 1918 to 1930.

But it would be hard to imagine a hero greater than Charles Lindbergh, a 25-year-old mail pilot who had begun his flying career as an aerial barnstormer, performing stunts and offering rides for $5 a trip. On the rainy morning of May 20, 1927, Lindbergh took off from Long Island's Roosevelt Field in the *Spirit of St. Louis*. He touched down 33½ hours later at Le Bourget airport, just north of Paris. Not only was Lindbergh the toast of the entire world, but his flight had a practical impact too. According to flight historian R.E.G. Davies, "the American people were suddenly seized with the idea that the aeroplane was a safe, speedy, and useful vehicle." By 1930 three commercial airlines were offering coast-to-coast flights.

The world was becoming a much smaller place. Cars were common enough that in 1925 the first motel opened, in San Luis Obispo, California. In 1926 the first transatlantic phone call went through, from New York to London.

But for all the giddiness and money and high spirits, there was something rotten at the core of the '20s. In fact, it began almost at the top. President Harding seems to have been an honest man himself, but a terrible judge of character. He had chosen as his secretary of the interior Albert Fall. In 1921 Fall persuaded the secretary of the navy to transfer control of the huge oil reserves in Teapot Dome, Wyoming, and Elk Hills, California, to the Department of the Interior. Fall then secretly leased the reserves to two oil companies in exchange for interest-free loans and outright cash gifts. Though acquitted of conspiracy charges, Fall was later convicted of accepting a bribe and served a year in prison. Harding died on August 2, 1923, two months before the scandal came to light. He was succeeded by his vice president, Calvin Coolidge, who was deemed to have been unaware of Fall's improprieties.

In his most famous utterance, Coolidge said that "the chief business of America is business." But in the late '20s Americans seemed more interested in speculation. Excited by tales of overnight fortunes, first-time investors poured not just their

The market crash produced hordes of worried investors awaiting word on the state of their dwindling fortunes.

discretionary incomes into the stock market, but also their savings and whatever additional funds they could beg and borrow. The economy was a house of cards. Having made erratic jumps and dips throughout the fall of 1929, the market suffered a selling spree on October 24 in which 13 million shares were dumped. Five days later the market crashed, with stocks losing an average of 40 points.

Herbert Hoover tried to reassure his panicked nation that "prosperity is just around the corner." Against the advice of his treasury secretary, he took a number of measures, urging businessmen to maintain prices and wages; offering tax cuts; and creating a variety of public works programs.

Nothing worked. The Depression deepened, with bread lines and shanty-filled "Hoovervilles" everywhere. No matter what measures he adopted,

Hoover was unable to bring the country out of its economic doldrums. Indeed, the Depression would last a decade, until Franklin Delano Roosevelt's New Deal brought a measure of relief.

The crash was an abrupt ending to a frenzied party. Summing up the event in 1931, Fitzgerald, probably the most perceptive critic of the era, wrote:

Somebody had blundered and the most expensive orgy in history was over.

It ended two years ago, because the utter confidence which was its essential prop received an enormous jolt, and it didn't take long for the flimsy structure to settle earthward. And after two years the Jazz Age seems as far away as the days before the War. It was borrowed time anyhow—the whole upper tenth of a nation living with the insouciance of grand ducs and the casualness of chorus girls.

PROHIBITION

A Michigan woman with 10 children received a life sentence for possessing a pint of gin, while Chicago's notorious Genna brothers operated a bootleg warehouse factory with impunity just four blocks from one of the city's largest police stations. In the nation's capital, congressmen voted "dry" but lived "wet"— slaking their tremendous thirst with illicit liquor stored by bootleggers in the House and Senate cellars. Such were the double standards that flourished for more than 13 years under Prohibition's largely unenforceable Volstead Act.

Approved by Congress in 1917 and ratified by two-thirds of the states two years later, the 18th Amendment to the Constitution went into effect at the stroke of midnight on January 17, 1920, despite President Wilson's opposition. While temperance advocates from the Anti-Saloon League of

America and the Women's Christian Temperance Union believed an "era of clear thinking and clean living" was at hand, former President William Taft rightly predicted that "the business of manufacturing alcohol, liquor and beer will go out of the hands of law-abiding members of the community and will be transferred to the quasi-criminal classes."

There was good reason for Taft's apprehension. From Portland, Oregon, to Portland, Maine, earlier local attempts to ban drinking had been flagrantly subverted. But the grass-roots popularity of Prohibition, based initially on medical arguments and later on moral and religious grounds, was unstoppable.

Prohibition not only made an institution of organized crime, but also criminalized the behavior of millions of Americans across class, gender

Confiscated booze (left) often ended up in the gutter, where Prohibition's moralistic proponents (above) thought it belonged.

"With Prohibition, America was all set for a wild drinking spree that would last thirteen years, five months, and nine days."

—*EDWARD BEHR,*
author of Prohibition, *1996*

The popularity of the home still (far left) increased despite the dangers inherent in the equipment: The 1925 explosion of a still in Norfolk, Massachusetts (opposite page, below), was thought to have killed five people. Police intercepted a rum-runner's cargo after a dramatic chase in New York Harbor (left). Federal agents Moe Smith and Izzy Einstein (above, left and right of still) were two of Prohibition's most famous enforcers.

and cultural lines. Even the usually sober middle class was carried away by the thrill of bathtub gin, hip flasks and home stills. For every saloon door that closed, a dozen illicit speakeasies opened. In New York City alone there were an estimated 100,000 speakeasies in 1926. Women, who had been among the chief proponents of temperance, flocked to 21 and the Stork Club to drink "the real McCoy"—unadulterated whiskey smuggled from the Bahamas by the infamous rumrunner and sailor Bill McCoy.

Those who could not afford to get "spifflicated" at speakeasies drank at home. In basements across the country, blocks of dried grapes were fermented to make wine. Beer drinkers converted "near beer" to a facsimile of the real thing by adding packages of yeast per brewers' instructions.

Americans turned to hard liquor as never before, and much of it was highly toxic. According to a Prohibition bureau report: "Of 480,000 gallons of confiscated booze analyzed in New York in 1927, 98 percent contained poisons." The 90-proof Jamaica ginger, or jake, caused partial paralysis of the extremities. Methanol, a deadly poison used to denature alcohol, was commonly found in hooch made from embalming fluid,

13

antifreeze solutions and rubbing alcohol. Tens of thousands of Americans died while exercising what they felt was their right to drink. But it would be years before the finger of blame was publicly pointed at the Volstead Act.

On the streets, Prohibition agents and local police were outnumbered and underpaid, inviting rampant corruption. Behind closed doors, legal loopholes that allowed for the production and sale of alcohol for medical and industrial purposes were exploited. In Chicago more than 15,000 doctors and 57,000 druggists applied for licences to sell "medicinal" liquor as soon as Volstead became

law—just one cog in the violent and corrupt machine run by mobster Al Capone and Mayor "Big Bill" Thompson. The corruption rose as high as President Harding's administration, where Attorney General Harry Daugherty and his sidekick Jess Smith reaped great spoils by selling immunity from prosecution to bootleggers.

Harding died suddenly in 1923 while in office; Smith committed suicide later that year; and

Women who frequented speakeasies (opposite page) often found ingenious ways to hide their booze (opposite page, below); some of them even became gin joint operators, such as Texas Guinan (left); members of the Busch family, Adolphus, August and August Jr. (left to right, below), celebrated the end of Prohibition by shipping a case of beer to President Roosevelt.

President Coolidge forced Daugherty to retire. But little changed until big business, one of Prohibition's most vocal early supporters, began lobbying for repeal of the Volstead Act to shift some of the tax burden from corporations back onto purchasers of alcohol. By the time the Depression hit, public support for Prohibition had withered and tax dollars were sorely needed. On December 6, 1932, President Franklin Roosevelt supported a resolution to nullify the 18th Amendment. A year later, with ratification by two-thirds of the states, Prohibition became the only amendment ever to be repealed.

Aftermath

The return of legally flowing real beer in America brought parades, processions and beer-tasting parties to the brewing capitals of Milwaukee and St. Louis. It also spelled the end of the "saloon" and the birth of the "bar." Major bootleggers continued to import and distribute the brands of liquor they formerly smuggled, and organized crime shifted its "protection" activities to storefront businesses such as restaurants and bakeries. The entrenchment of organized crime is perhaps Prohibition's most enduring legacy.

MARGARET MEAD

From her tower office at New York City's American Museum of Natural History, from the lecture podium at Columbia University and, later, from her exalted perch on the television talk-show circuit, anthropologist Margaret Mead turned her studies of far-off cultures into talking points for modern American society.

Mead began observing the behavior of other people at a very young age. Under her grandmother's tutelage, she took notes on how her younger sisters' vocabularies developed, just as her mother had taken notes on Margaret after her birth on December 16, 1901, in Philadelphia.

Mead's parents were hardworking, free-thinking educators. They instilled in Margaret—the oldest of four—a strong work ethic and a well-developed sense of independence that would impel her toward a fully articulated feminism as she grew older. Where Mead got her desire for fame is less certain. But that she became one of the most in-

fluential women of her generation was no twist of fate or act of God. She planned it. "I'm going to be famous some day and I'm going to be known by my own name," Mead declared as a Columbia University student embarking on the first of her three marriages.

She had the good fortune to enter the field of anthropology in the early '20s, when the need to document vanishing cultures was at its most urgent. And after receiving her master's degree from Columbia in 1924, she set off with her boundless energy and intellectual agility to study the sexual behavior of adolescent girls on the South Pacific island of Samoa. Her reports of sexually permissive and carefree Samoans challenged the prevailing view that adolescent angst was biologically determined and thus inevitable. Over time, critics would argue that Mead was misled by her belief in cultural determinism. True or not, the publication of Mead's findings in

Mead's work with Samoan children (left) and with third husband Gregory Bateson (above) made her a household name.

"**Children are our vehicles for survival—for in them there is hope, and through them what has been and what will be will not only be perpetuated, but also united.**"

—*Margaret Mead*

Mead was able to draw significant implications for American society from her work with children (opposite page) and her fascination with the paraphernalia of foreign cultures (left).

Coming of Age in Samoa (1928)—which suggested that Americans too could move happily through adolescence if only unfettered by cultural baggage—captivated the nation and catapulted the 27-year-old Mead onto the lecture and media circuits. It also marked the arrival of Mead's signature style of comparing far-off cultures to American society.

Her success was particularly notable in light of the sometimes virulent strains of nativism that infected the United States body politic in the '20s and '30s. A powerful alternative voice, Mead elo-

quently suggested that cultures beyond our borders had much to teach us.

Awarded her Ph.D. in 1929, Mead spent much of the next 10 years conducting field studies in New Guinea and Bali, working initially alongside her second husband, Reo Fortune, and later with her third, Gregory Bateson. During this period Mead made lasting advances in field research methods, pioneered the use of photography—with Bateson—and wrote *Growing up in New Guinea* and *Sex and Temperament in Three Primitive Societies,* which fo-

would be popularized by Benjamin Spock, the pediatrician Mead chose in part because he had undergone psychoanalysis.

cused on child-rearing practices and gender roles.

When Mead's and Bateson's daughter, Cathy, was born in 1939, the influence of the "Mother to the World," as Mead would later be called by *Time* magazine, only grew. Well ahead of her time, she breast-fed on demand—a practice she had observed in primitive cultures and one that

Just as Mead designed a life that extended well beyond the bounds of the "nuclear family"—relying heavily on a vast network of friends and family whose lives she was known to direct as consciously as her own—she considered the entire world to be her field of study. "It's all anthropology," she once said. In the words of her protégé Lenora Foerstel,

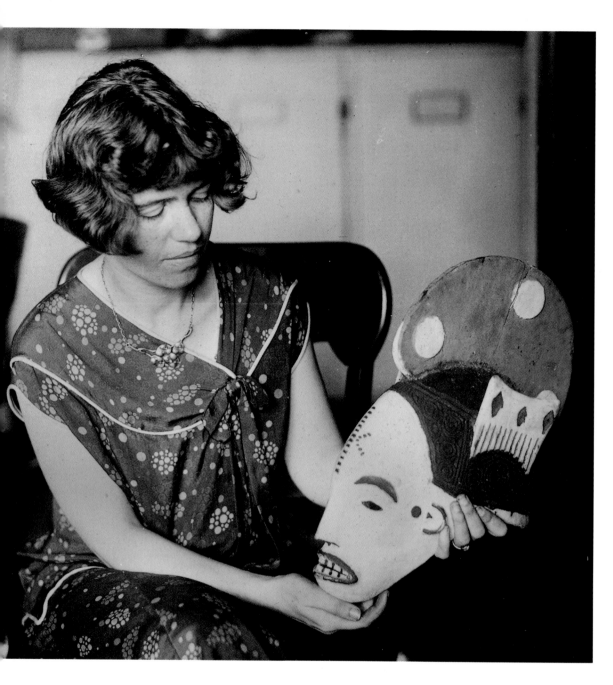

Mead struck an odd figure, surrounded by native peoples such as the ceremonial dancers above. Over the years, she continued to collect cultural artifacts (left), many of which became part of a major exhibit dedicated to Pacific Island cultures at New York City's Museum of Natural History in 1971 (opposite page).

"Her greatest forte was getting the right minds together to explain how interdisciplinary ideas could dovetail." But Mead's position as celebrity anthropologist and authority on everything from overpopulation, nutrition and education to sexual stereotypes and nuclear politics alienated academic purists. It also left little room for Bateson, who moved out in 1948 and divorced Mead in 1950.

When Mead died on November 15, 1978, she had 34 books and more than 1,300 articles and other published works to her credit. Despite the controversy that continues to swirl around her research in Samoa, much of what Mead said, wrote and did as a groundbreaking anthropologist, steadfast friend and social, moral and political authority resonates in contemporary conversation.

Aftermath

Coming of Age in Samoa is the best-selling anthropology text of all time. Although Dr. Mead received 28 honorary degrees, she was never elected to the National Academy of Sciences. Still, her pioneering work in areas such as learning theory and mental imprinting are of great interest today. Her most lasting contributions were the links she forged between anthropology and other fields, notably psychology. Today, interdisciplinary studies are common, and generations of Americans have learned to understand the complexities of human nature better by studying other cultures. Whatever may be disputed about Mead's work, she can certainly be credited with permanently energizing and popularizing her field.

BABE RUTH

In 1961, when Roger Maris was chasing Babe Ruth's single-season record of 60 home runs, former A's infielder Jimmy Dykes remarked, "Maris is a fine ballplayer, but I can't imagine him driving down Broadway in a low-slung convertible, wearing a coonskin coat."

No, and the red silk robe and slippers the Babe often lounged in probably wouldn't have suited Maris, either. Though Maris did break Ruth's mark that season, cracking 61 homers, and in 1974 Hank Aaron surpassed the Babe's career total of 714 homers, Ruth still holds plenty of records, and his legend, like his career slugging average of .690, has not been approached. He remains not only a baseball star but also an icon of American culture. As the ultimate insult to their U.S. enemies during World War II, Japanese troops would shout, "To hell with Babe Ruth!"

The exploits of George Herman Ruth, like those of all legendary figures, were always embellished—by the press, the public and the man himself—obscuring the line between truth and fantasy. Did Ruth really "call" his famous home run in the 1932 World Series®? Did he truly promise a homer to a dying, hospitalized boy, the delivery of which prompted the lad's swift recovery? Did he in fact dangle Yankees manager Miller Huggins off the end of a train by his heels? Maybe; not exactly; and definitely not, are the respective answers to those questions, but such gray areas are part of the Babe's mystique. Even Ruth's birth date is a matter of debate: He insisted he was born on February 7, 1894, but records in Baltimore cite February 6, 1895. Legend has it that he grew up in an orphanage; the truth is that his parents sent him as an "incorrigible" to St. Mary's Indus-

Ruth's prodigious appetites—including one for cigars, which he sold himself (above)—helped make him a legend.

"I had a better year than he did."

—BABE RUTH, in 1930, upon being told that his $80,000 salary exceeded that of President Herbert Hoover.

trial School for Boys when he was 10. Ruth was there off and on until he was 20.

Whatever tall tales exist in Ruth's story, it is clear that, once released from the Catholic reformatory in 1914 to join the local minor league team, the Baltimore Orioles, he tore through life at full tilt. His drinking and womanizing were immeasurable, as was his generosity. Of Ruth's appetite for food, former teammate Ernie Shore could only say, "Oh, my God. Oh, lord-a-mighty."

Ruth got his nickname from his fellow Orioles, who called him "Dunn's Babe" after Jack Dunn, the owner of the team, who had taken legal custody of Ruth upon his release from St. Mary's. And the Babe was an immediate success. A left-handed pitcher with a blazing fastball, he could also hit for

Ruth's major league ca-
reer began with the Red
Sox (opposite page), who
sold him to the Yankees,
for whom he played in the
Polo Grounds (opposite
page, top) before the team
moved to Yankee Stadium
(left); the photo at left was
the basis for a postage
stamp in 1983; Ruth's love
of stunts led him to partic-
ipate in a 1931 fungo contest (above) in which he
drove the ball 422 feet
with the narrow bat.

Ruth's legendary affection for children (above) may have derived from the important role played in his own life by teachers such as Brother Benjamin (left) from St. Mary's.

power. In his first game as a professional, an intrasquad scrimmage in Fayetteville, North Carolina, Ruth hit a home run so prodigious it made headlines in the local papers, which said the blast exceeded the longest one ever hit on that field, by another American hero, Jim Thorpe.

Financial pressures forced Dunn to sell Ruth to the Boston Red Sox that July, and, after a stint in the Sox farm system, the next year the young hurler broke into the majors, where he won 18 games and helped lead Boston to its third World Series® championship, which it successfully de-

fended the following season. In 1917 Ruth established himself as the best lefty in baseball by winning 24 games. In the next year's Fall Classic he pitched a record 29⅔ scoreless innings, leading Boston to victory over the Chicago Cubs. Yet Ruth's bat was so fearsome that the Sox made him an everyday player in 1919, and he hit an unprecedented 29 home runs that season. Much to the chagrin of Boston fans, team owner Harry Frazee, deep in debt, sold the Bambino to the Yankees in December 1919. He got $125,000 for the slugger. The Red Sox have not won a World Series® since.

Ruth electrified baseball his first year in New York by hitting 54 home runs. In 1921 he hit 59. Enough fans flocked to see him that in 1923 the Yankees could afford to construct a new park,

Ruth's status as cultural icon led to commercial endorsements and even songs (bottom); Ruth gave Lou Gehrig an affectionate hug (below) after Gehrig's 1939 farewell at Yankee Stadium; in 1948 a frail Ruth (right) also bade farewell—just two months later he was dead.

"It gives an errorless shave
and hits 1,000 in smoothness, comfort, speed"

Barbasol
For Modern Shaving

"BATTERIN' BABE"
"LOOK AT HIM NOW"
THE HOME RUN SONG HIT OF THE SEASON

Dedicated to
OUR OWN
BABE RUTH

WORDS
JACK O'BRIEN
MUSIC
BILLY TIMMINS

Published by
COLONIAL MUSIC PUBLISHING CO

Yankee Stadium, soon to be known as the House that Ruth Built. Ruth hit the first home run in the stadium. He hit 40 more that year, had a .393 batting average and led the Yankees to their first World Series® title. He topped the league in homers every year from 1926 to 1931. In 1927 Ruth hit 60 home runs, batted .356 and drove in 138 runs.

For many, however, Ruth's Called Shot against the Cubs remains the centerpiece of his legend, and rightly so, for the moment was a beguiling mix of mastery and mystery. Did he truly point to the center-field fence before he blasted the ball far over that spot? The Babe had a simple answer: "It's in the papers, isn't it?"

Aftermath

Ruth, who appeared on seven World Series®-winning teams (three in Boston, four in New York), retired in 1935. He had left the Yankees that year and signed as a player-vice president with the Boston Braves in the hope of becoming a manager. When it became clear that the organization did not consider him managerial material, Ruth retired, having competed in 28 games for the Braves. His final flourish came early that season, when he hit three home runs in a game against Pittsburgh. The third, Ruth's 714th and last homer, cleared the roof of the upper deck in right field at Forbes Field. Estimated to have traveled 600 feet, it was the longest homer ever hit in that ballpark.

Ruth died of throat cancer in 1948 at age 53.

THE GATSBY STYLE

There was music from my neighbor's house through the summer nights. In his blue gardens men and girls came and went like moths among the whisperings and the champagne and the stars.

The lights grow brighter as the earth lurches away from the sun and now the orchestra is playing yellow cocktail music and the opera of voices pitches a key higher. Laughter is easier, minute by minute, spilled with prodigality, tipped out at a cheerful word.

— F. Scott Fitzgerald
The Great Gatsby

F. Scott Fitzgerald, who christened the Jazz Age and served as its poet and critic, composed some of the most elegant, evocative, musical prose ever written. *The Great Gatsby*, which he wrote while touring Europe in 1924 and 1925 and published in April 1925, is his masterpiece. T. S. Eliot had spelled out the spiritual emptiness of the times a few years earlier in his ambitious poem *The Waste Land*, and Ernest Hemingway would explore the hollow lives of what Gertrude Stein called the Lost Generation in *The Sun Also Rises*, which was published in 1926.

But it was *Gatsby* that took the fluttering pulse of America during the years between the Great War and the Depression better than any other work. It is the story of Nick Carraway, a young Midwesterner who goes East to seek his fortune as a bond trader in New York City. He rents a cottage on the north shore of Long Island and winds up forming a friendship of sorts with his wealthy neighbor, the mysterious Jay Gatsby.

In describing Gatsby's extraordinarily lavish parties, Nick, Fitzgerald's narrator, shows us the hedonistic world of the idle rich. Viewed through the bottom of one of Gatsby's champagne glasses,

Fitzgerald (left, with wife Zelda and daughter Scottie) was the premier chronicler of the high-spirited '20s (above).

it is a shimmering, diaphanous place, filled with sleek expensive cars, tuxedos, raccoon coats and hip flasks worn by women who have no hips.

Money was everywhere in the '20s, more of it than ever before, and fun was pursued around the clock with almost hysterical intensity. Jazz meant sex long before it meant music, but in the '20s the distinction was blurred like everything else. "By 1926," Fitzgerald wrote in an essay, "the universal preoccupation with sex had become a nuisance."

No writer has ever made money look as alluring as Fitzgerald does. But just beneath the surface of his prose is a wasteland every bit as depressing as Eliot's:

The bar is in full swing and floating rounds of cocktails permeate the garden outside until the air is alive with chatter and laughter and causal innuendo and introductions forgotten on the spot and enthusiastic meetings between women who never knew each other's names.

For all his pretensions, Gatsby turns out to have a sordid past, and when he pressures Nick to introduce him to Nick's married cousin Daisy Buchanan, Gatsby's gorgeous world comes crashing down. In the end, Fitzgerald's verdict on Daisy and her husband, Tom, seems to sum up his conclusion about their entire social set:

They were careless people, Tom and Daisy— they smashed up things and creatures and then retreated back into their money or their vast carelessness or whatever it was that kept them together, and let other people clean up the mess they had made.

More than anything else, perhaps, the Gatsby style meant men in top hats and tails and women in sleek flapper attire attending elegant parties that stretched endlessly into the night.

"It was borrowed time anyhow—the whole upper
tenth of the nation living with the insouciance of
grand dues and the casualness of chorus girls."
—F. SCOTT FITZGERALD, in "Echoes of the Jazz Age," 1931

31

Fitzgerald's ambivalence about the rich ran deep. Born in St. Paul, Minnesota, in 1896, he was named for one of his ancestors, national anthem composer Francis Scott Key. During Fitzgerald's boyhood his father's furniture business failed, but the family was able to fall back on his mother's inheritance. Fitzgerald was sent East to boarding school, and then to Princeton, where he neglected his studies in favor of writing skits and lyrics for the drama club and taking his first stab at fiction.

When it became clear that he would not graduate, Fitzgerald joined the army. While stationed at Camp Sheridan in Alabama, he met Zelda Sayre, an 18-year-old belle, at a country club dance in Montgomery. In 1920, a week after Fitzgerald's autobiographical first novel, *This Side of Paradise*, was published to great acclaim, the two were married. Roughly paralleling the fortunes of their boom decade, Scott and Zelda had 10 good, wild years together, indulging in drink and all the other vices of the Jazz Age, before their lives collapsed in the early '30s.

Ernst Dryden's illustration (opposite page, below) captured the languid elegance of the Gatsby set; the roadsters in which the elite shuttled from party to party included Mercedes (left), Studebakers (opposite page) and Oaklands (below).

Their reckoning was a heavy one. Zelda spent most of her adult life in and out of asylums, getting treatment for schizophrenia, and Fitzgerald died of a heart attack in 1940 at the age of 44, convinced he was a failure.

He was wrong, of course. Reading the final lines of *The Great Gatsby*—surely one of the finest endings to any novel of any generation—one is hard-pressed to imagine anyone else capturing so beautifully the yearning that seems so fundamentally American and the reality that thwarts it:

Gatsby believed in the green light, the orgastic future that year by year recedes before us. It eluded us then, but that's no matter—tomorrow we will run faster, stretch out our arms farther.... And one fine morning—

So we beat on, boats against the current, borne back ceaselessly into the past.

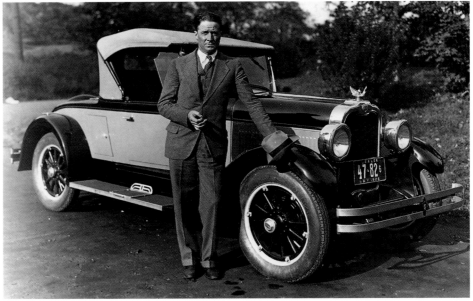

Aftermath

In the library of his new $100 million home, Microsoft mogul Bill Gates has inscribed on the wall Fitzgerald's sympathetic take on Jay Gatsby: "He had come a long way to this blue lawn and his dream must have seemed so close he could hardly fail to grasp it."

33

EARLY RADIO

Viewed from today's information superhighways, the early days of American radio look like scenic but dusty country roads. Indeed, tales of broadcasts being disturbed by roaring trains or preempted by ship-to-shore distress signals abound. Yet, in less than a decade, transmitting sound waves through the ether grew from the occasional hobbyist's garage experiment into a billion-dollar industry that linked 40 percent of America's 123 million inhabitants.

Just as several turn-of-the-century inventors claimed to be the father of radio (in 1943 the Supreme Court awarded the title to Nikola Tesla of Serbia, who secured a wireless-related patent in 1898), various people took credit for transmitting the first commercial broadcast. The first transmission to generate real interest in radio, though, came on November 2, 1920, when KDKA reported the presidential election returns from a makeshift shed on the roof of the West-

inghouse Electric building in East Pittsburgh. Fewer than 1,000 receivers picked up the broadcast of Warren Harding's victory over James Cox, but word of the wireless spread fast.

By 1921, bulky, battery-operated sets—called wireless music boxes, wireless telephones or radio telephones—had found their way into 60,000 homes. Stations were popping up everywhere. Poultry farmers, car dealers, electric companies, newspaper publishers and religious cultists all took to the airwaves, hoping to convert listeners to their products, services or beliefs.

There were more than 550 stations and an estimated 1.5 million households with sets by 1923. Overlapping signals and lack of regulation created chaos. To avoid jamming, entire cities observed self-imposed "silent nights." In Chicago, for instance, stations shut down on Mondays, in Dallas on Wednesdays. Listeners often did not

AT&T's J. P. Maloy broadcast the 1924 World Series® live, a treat no doubt for early listeners like the boys above.

know what was on when. When they could tune in, they struggled to hear chatter, music, sports and two-bit comedy routines through a cacophony of crackles and pops.

Many early radio personalities played the piano under one name, then read the news under another. And while big-name entertainers did make appearances, stations on shoestring budgets depended far more on local performers such as Lawrence Welk, who got his start playing accordion for WNAX of the Gurney Seed and Nursery Company in Yankton, South Dakota. The novelty of the medium easily compensated for its pro-

gramming and technical shortcomings, and nobody was offended when bands were given names such as The Lucky Strike Orchestra, The Ipana Troubadours and the A&P Gypsies, to sell cigarettes, toothpaste and groceries, respectively.

Credit for radio's swift evolution into a communications and entertainment behemoth goes largely to David Sarnoff, the engineer-turned-president of the Radio Corporation of America (RCA), who recognized radio's tremendous potential when, as a wireless operator in New York City, he picked up distress signals from the sinking *Titanic* and broadcast the names of survivors

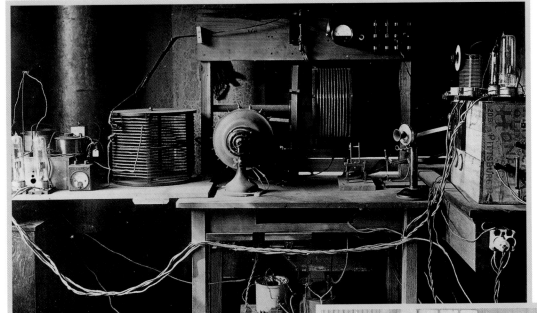

Despite their invisibility, early radio performers (opposite page) often dressed for their parts; the home of Westinghouse's Dr. Frank Conrad (below, left) was the site of early radio experiments, and KDKA's first transmitter (left) was built there; the first notable broadcast (below) delivered the 1920 presidential election results to the nation.

"Radio was so easy; if you could read your lines without rattling the paper, you were a great star."

—*GEORGE BURNS,*
comedian

for 72 straight hours. In 1923, RCA, the biggest supplier of transmitters, teamed up with the American Telephone and Telegraph Company (AT&T), whose phone wires could carry signals for simultaneous broadcast by affiliates. The era of networks was born. When, driven by cries of monopoly, AT&T bowed out in 1926, RCA simply formed a new company called the National Broadcasting Company (NBC), which went on to rent phone wires from AT&T.

NBC's first network broadcast, in 1926, brought live performances from New York City, Chicago and Independence, Kansas, to 19 stations and 10 million listeners across the United States via 3,600 miles of telephone wire. The feat prompted millions of Americans to purchase radios. In the decade's remaining years, radio turned the Scopes trial, Charles Lindbergh's transatlantic flight, the St. Valentine's Day Massacre and other notable events into national sto-

As radio's popularity grew, a variety of models became available in retail outlets (left) and the radio appeared in more and more locales, including cars (opposite page), barns (right) and, of course, in living rooms, where the medium attracted listeners of every sort (below).

ries. When the stock market crashed in 1929, people heard the news first on their radios.

On a lighter note, by the early '30s Jack Benny's jokes and Bing Crosby's crooning had become fixtures in American households. And the nightly broadcast of *Amos 'n' Andy*, the most popular radio show of all time, provided 40 million Americans with a common experience—something no movie theater, speakeasy, newspaper or phonograph record could do.

Aftermath

The advent of recording tape in the 1940s brought big changes to radio. Shows could be taped anywhere, at any time. And they could be edited. Live music, initially radio's main attraction, was tape's first casualty. The biggest blows to radio, though, came with the arrival of television in the '40s. By the early '60s the radio serials, series and comedy shows that had united millions of Americans had all but vanished.

Today, sports, news, talk shows and recorded music are the medium's mainstays. Though radio is no longer the nation's great unifier, it still thrives. According to Eric Rhoads, publisher of *Radio Ink:* "About 98 percent of Americans listen to radio every week. And the average American listens three-plus hours a week."

ART DECO STYLE

A streamlined architecture of zigzagging terraces and towering ziggurats. Traditional office buildings exuberantly ornamented with sunburst motifs, flowered reliefs, leaping gazelles and flamingos. Geometric and pragmatic structures reaching the sky thanks to new developments in steel construction and reinforced concrete. This was Art Deco.

The term was coined in the 1960s as a shorthand reference to the style introduced at the 1925 Exposition Internationale des Arts Décoratifs et Industriels Modernes in Paris. Opulent and extravagant, Art Deco introduced art nouveau, cubism, futurism, Egyptian influences and an appreciation for modern technology into every area of the decorative arts. It merged the straight lines of the Bauhaus and International styles with highly ornamental elements of the Viennese Secession, and mirrored the era's sense of rhythm and excitement.

Though the new style was incorporated into everything from ceramics to painting to glasswork and furniture in both Europe and the United States, Art Deco made its biggest mark in American architecture. Art Deco's arrival here coincided with a period of explosive growth in the construction of office buildings— or cathedrals of commerce, as they were nicknamed. The two were a perfect match: the exuberant Art Deco style emphasized the new heights of power and wealth that United States corporations reached, while the towering skyscrapers those companies were building provided ideal backdrops for the new, highly ornamental style. New York City, the nation's capital of commerce,

South Miami Beach (above) and New York's Chrysler Building (left) are classic examples of Art Deco style.

41

The stainless steel arches (far left) and triangular windows (left) of the Chrysler Building's spire (above and left middle) and the 59th-floor gargoyles (opposite page, right) are even more eye-catching than the architect's model (opposite page, left) envisioned.

emerged as the proving ground for Art Deco.

The most notable of New York's cathedrals of commerce is the Chrysler Building, designed by William van Alen for automobile magnate Walter P. Chrysler. At the time, Chrysler wanted to build the tallest building in the world, a shrine not only to his own success but also to capitalism itself. As he said at the building's dedication ceremony in 1930, "The Chrysler Building is dedicated to the world of commerce and industry ... as a sound contribution to business progress."

It was the building's ornamentation rather than its structure that made the 77 floors of rental office space classic. Eagle gargoyles of chromium-nickel steel jazz up the 59th-floor setback, while on the 31st floor exterior, "car wheels" made of colored brick with metal "hubcaps" serve promotional and decorative purposes. The building's 27-ton spire, adorned with stainless steel arches and triangular windows, still stands out in the crowded Manhattan skyline.

For a very short time, the Chrysler Building stretched farther into the sky than any building in the world. At 1,046 feet, it eclipsed its rival Bank of Manhattan at 40 Wall Street by 119 feet and the Eiffel Tower by 60 feet. But Chrysler en-

"**Walk up New York's Lexington Avenue and gaze at the silvery spire of the Chrysler Building: one can feel the messages of power, technology, exotica, and elegance shimmering down from the ziggurat atop the skyline.**"
—*RICHARD STRINER, author, 1994*

joyed this status for less than a year. In 1931 the Empire State Building checked in at 1,250 feet, but it could not compare to the Chrysler in terms of modernist ornamentation.

The Art Deco explosion gradually spread across the country. Department stores such as Bullock's in Los Angeles and national chains like Sears and Woolworth's incorporated the style into their architecture, interior designs and advertising. Supermarkets, shopping centers, cinemas, drive-ins and diners would soon follow. Entire towns were fashioned in the style. The streamlined, pastel stucco buildings of South Miami Beach, Florida,

with their seashell and flamingo ornamentation, are classic examples of regionalized Art Deco. Even a town as remote from the style's place of origin as Napier, New Zealand, which had been destroyed by an earthquake in 1931, was rebuilt in the Art Deco style.

The construction of Art Deco buildings began to taper off as the Depression set in, and ended with the advent of World War II. But its lavish ornamentation, considered out of place in the new decade of difficult times, remains a strong reminder of the optimism of the 1920s.

The Art Deco style, which spread from New York to cities such as Miami (above, left), was incorporated in the design of chairs and other furnishings (above) as well as interior details, like bannisters (above, right) and clocks (right).

Aftermath

The Art Deco architectural style experienced a strong revival in the late 1970s and early '80s. Evidence of its Renaissance can be seen in structures around the country, such as the Public Services Building (1980–1982) in Portland, Oregon, the High Museum of Art (1980–1983) in Atlanta, and the One Liberty Place office tower (1986) in Philadelphia. The spirit of Art Deco has survived most of all, however, in furniture, ceramics, and other decorative pieces, all of which reflect an energetic past and a spirited notion of futuristic design.

Hot Five,
Record Artists

JAZZ EXPLOSION

The year was 1927, the setting the glittery Cotton Club on Harlem's Lenox Avenue. Duke Ellington and his band were onstage, turning out sizzling jazz for an audience of the rich and powerful. The bootlegged liquor flowed openly while politicians rubbed shoulders with foreign dignitaries and local gangsters. From this last group came a request. Jack (Legs) Diamond wanted to hear *St. Louis Blues*. Ellington complied. Legs left his table to dance near the stage. When the song was over Diamond repeated his request, and continued to do so into the wee hours. Ellington played *St. Louis Blues* all night long. As dawn approached, Diamond told Duke, "Buy yourself a cigar!" and handed over a $1,000 bill, then another, and walked out the door.

Such dizzying scenes were not uncommon in the Roaring Twenties, and they provided ample evidence of jazz's rise, like bubbles in a champagne glass, from its humble beginnings in the Mississippi Delta. Like its slightly older cousin, the blues, jazz emerged from the ashes of slavery, borrowing rhythmic and improvisational elements from work songs and spirituals.

By the late 1880s brass dance and concert bands—often using instruments cast off by Civil War military bands—were performing in most southern cities. The epicenter of the emerging form was New Orleans. With its open social atmosphere, the Crescent City provided a gumbo of ethnic and cultural backgrounds, and it was the ideal breeding ground for jazz, a form that borrowed from, and reconciled, disparate sources—classical music, African rhythms, traditional spirituals, ragtime and blues. Buddy Bolden, Joe (King) Oliver, Jelly Roll Morton and Louis Armstrong all gave daily life in New Or-

Oliver (above, with cornet) and Armstrong (opposite page, second from left) were two of the greatest jazz popularizers.

leans its own jazz score, and became legends in the process.

Oliver, the king of Big Easy cornetists, took his band to Chicago in 1918, joining a mass northern migration to wartime industrial jobs. His protégé, Armstrong, stayed behind to play trumpet for a Mississippi riverboat band until Oliver sent for him four years later. By 1922 jazz was flourishing in Chicago. Speakeasies and nightclubs that stayed open till dawn dotted the city. Al Capone, whom Armstrong later remem-

bered as "a nice little cute fat boy," made the scene with his henchmen.

It was here that Armstrong began his ascent to the pantheon of jazz performers. His command of his instrument complete, and his soloing increasingly innovative, Armstrong graduated in 1924 to Fletcher Henderson's outfit, acknowledged as the best jazz band in the nation. The group now had the top trumpeter in the world, "head and shoulders above them all," as one colleague put it. In 1924 Armstrong moved with

The modest facade of the original Cotton Club (left) in Harlem belied the vast talents, such as Ellington (opposite page), who worked within; Beiderbecke (below, with cornet) was among the top white jazz artists of the era.

Henderson's band to New York, where he remained the focus of the jazz world.

Though black musicians invented jazz, the genre attracted a large white audience—the first black art form to do so. Indeed, Armstrong was the first black star of any kind to "cross over" to a white audience. But jazz had more than a few proficient white practitioners as well. Among these were Bix Beiderbecke, the talented trumpeter from Iowa who died at 28; George Gershwin, whose music, while not tech-

"Jazz didn't come up the river from New Orleans. It took the Illinois Central Railroad....It came in box-back coats and high-button shoes, with clarinet sticking out of back pocket and trombone wrapped in newspaper."

—*FRANK DRIGGS AND HARRIS LEWINE, authors, Black Beauty, White Heat, 1982*

nically jazz, contained jazz elements, and greatly increased the music's popularity; and orchestra leader Paul Whiteman, who, using the proceeds from his enormous record sales, secured the very best white players—very few bands of the era were integrated—including Beiderbecke and Tommy and Jimmy Dorsey. With Whiteman's orchestra downtown, Ellington's and Henderson's acts uptown, and jazz-influenced productions on Broadway, the new music had thoroughly enveloped New York City. Europe was listening, too. In a matter of decades, jazz had

become America's most significant indigenous art form.

Chicago, meanwhile, continued to thrive, and in Kansas City, "the Paris of the Plains," a lively scene had developed. Armstrong, who by the mid-1920s had emerged as a vocalist and showman as well, returned to Chicago in 1926 to play the Dreamland Club for a handsome $75 a week. Morton took his propulsive Red Hot Peppers up to Chicago from New Orleans. Ellington stayed on at the Cotton Club until 1933, ushering in the swinging big-band era. Jazz was here to stay.

Aftermath

The swing era, led by Ellington and Count Basie, lasted into the mid-1940s, when improvisation moved to the fore. During the music's Golden Age, from 1935 to 1955, New York's West 52nd Street became the center of the jazz world. Playing Manhattan was so lucrative that jazz musicians dubbed the city "the Big Apple." Over the years a variety of jazz styles—among them bebop, cool, modern and free form—developed, each of which has survived in its own right, a testament to the vitality of the art form.

The jazz-infused music of Gershwin (above) and the success of Whiteman and his band (top) helped jazz cross over to white audiences and make legends of black performers such as Morton (above, right) and Cab Calloway (opposite page, with baton).

EMILY POST'S *ETIQUETTE*

The 700-page manual offered Dos and Don'ts for every social occasion. Do place the fish fork directly to the left of the meat fork. Don't congratulate a bride on hooking a husband. Do bring a chaperone to a portrait-painting session. And when chancing upon a former spouse, don't act familiar. Rather, greet him as a total stranger.

First published in 1922, Emily Post's *Etiquette: The Blue Book of Social Usage* gamely took on questions of table settings, mourning habits, visiting cards and household help. And despite its debut in a decade that questioned strictures on social customs ranging from courtship and marriage to drinking and dress, the book was an immediate and stunning success.

Though one of Post's employees would later suggest that *Etiquette* was written "to tell people who had made large fortunes in World War I

what to do with their new footmen, coachmen and chambermaids," it actually spoke to an audience that extended far beyond the wealthy. With sympathy rather than condescension, Post helped a burgeoning, and somewhat perplexed, middle class decode society's "standards." And, using fictional families such as the Oldworlds, the Onceweres, the Highbrows and the Wellborns, she brought a measure of fun to the proceedings.

Fifty-one at the time of the book's release, Post maintained that manners were nothing more than "a sensitive awareness of the needs of others." Perhaps it was this simple, unswerving belief that accounted for *Etiquette*'s endurance through decades of social change. For 38 years, until she died in 1960, Post reigned as America's Doyenne of Decorum, revising her tome 10 times, seeing it reprinted 89 times, writing a syndicated newspaper column

Post (above, left) dictated her weekly advice column and always cut an appropriately stylish figure (opposite page).

"Breakfast bacon should, when possible, be eaten with a fork. But when it is so dry and crisp that it scatters into fragments... fingers are permitted...."

—*EMILY POST,* Etiquette: The Blue Book of Social Usage, *1922*

that elicited thousands of letters a month, and hosting a daily radio show.

Post could hardly have envisioned her life following such a course. Born in 1872 to distinguished architect Bruce Price and his wife, Josephine, Emily spent her childhood shuttling between exclusive residences in Manhattan and Tuxedo Park, New York. She turned to writing full time only after her divorce from Edwin Post in 1905. Post had lost his fortune in the panic of 1901, and the divorce left Emily with two young sons and no substantial means of support.

She published her first novel, *The Flight of the Moth*, in 1904, and over the next two decades produced numerous essays, short stories and six more novels, all of them peppered with examples of proper social behavior—observations that came naturally from someone "to the manner born." Thus, when Post scoffed at a Funk & Wagnalls editor's suggestion that she write a book on etiquette, the editor understandably protested, "But

your books are full of nothing else!" Post went home and wrote 250,000 words in 10 months.

There was almost no question of conduct the Doyenne refused to tackle. "You may have had a successful hunting trip and wish to send the President a brace of pheasants," she wrote in *Etiquette*'s Washington section. Post cautioned against doing so, noting the Secret Service's dislike of small packages.

Changing with the times did not always come easily to Post. As *Newsweek* observed in its obituary of the writer, she was "imbued with a streak of Victorianism as obvious as a diamond tiara, and her sense of fitness about things was easily and usually outraged by innovation." Yet the magazine added that Post "knew she couldn't referee 20th century conduct with 19th century rules." *Etiquette*'s various editions consequently serve as milestones in the evolution of national mores. A 1937 revision to the question, "May a woman pursue a man?" allowed the following:

"Catlike, she may do a little stalking. But run? Not a step.... One who bounds in pursuit, like a puppy let loose, has lost the prize at the start!"

When Elizabeth Post, Emily's daughter-in-law, took *Etiquette*'s helm in 1955, the book continued to break new ground. Premarital sex and women's liberation were introduced as subjects in 1975. A section on the "etiquette of intimacy" in the most recent edition—published in 1997, and edited by Emily's great-granddaughter-in-law Peggy Post— responds to the onset of AIDS. The '97 edition also includes lists of holy days from Hindu to Quaker, and suggestions for what a woman who has chosen to bear a child on her own should tell her offspring. "If she was artificially inseminated," Peggy writes, "the mother should say to her child, 'I chose to have you because I wanted to love you and give you a happy life.' "

And if former spouses meet? "They should act as friendly and normal as possible."

Etiquette '22, meet the etiquette of the '90s.

Aftermath

Emily Post's Etiquette has weathered competition from Amy Vanderbilt, Letitia Baldridge, Miss Manners and other paragons of proper behavior to remain the best-selling title in its category 76 years after the book's initial publication.

Apparently, there's a need to fill. In a national survey conducted by *U.S. News and World Report* in 1996, 78 percent of respondents maintained that incivility had worsened in the previous decade, and nearly 90 percent considered it "a serious problem."

Read up, America.

EDWARD HOPPER

"If you could say it in words, there'd be no reason to paint," the famously taciturn Edward Hopper once said. The master of American realism nonetheless spoke volumes about the emptiness of modern life in this country throughout his 60-year career.

Born on July 22, 1882, to a solidly middle-class family in the Hudson River town of Nyack, New York, Eddie, as he was called, began signing and dating his drawings at the age of 10. By the time he turned 40, though, he had sold only one painting, and had to support himself as an illustrator, a job he disliked immensely.

Hopper's early years were characterized by a struggle to assimilate the influences of French culture and painting he witnessed during three trips to Paris from 1906 to 1910. Although he did eventually distance himself from the short, choppy brushstrokes and the light, bright palette of Impressionism, he insisted on showing his French paintings in New York City at a time when nativist work was in vogue, bringing upon himself economic and artistic hardship.

Hopper's breakthrough came in 1923, when his friend, fellow artist and future wife, Josephine (Jo) Nivison, persuaded the Brooklyn Museum to include some of Hopper's watercolors in a group show. At the time Hopper had all but given up oils in favor of watercolors and etchings. Critics raved and the museum bought

Both *Nighthawks* (above) and *House by the Railroad* (opposite page) convey Hopper's central theme of solitude.

Edward Hopper, Automat, *1927, oil on canvas, 28⅛ x 36 inches, Des Moines Art Center Permanent Collection, 1958.2*

"It is hard to think of another painter who is getting more of the quality of America in his canvases than Edward Hopper."

—LLOYD GOODRICH, art historian and critic, 1927

The Mansard Roof for $100. It was the first painting Hopper had sold in 10 years.

He and Nivison wed on July 9, 1924, and Hopper had his first one-man show at a commercial venue, the Frank K. M. Rehn Gallery, that year. All 11 watercolors exhibited sold, in addition to five that were not in the show. Confident and financially able to devote more time to painting, Hopper went

back to oils. In 1929, the newly opened Museum of Modern Art included six of his canvases in its first show of contemporary American art.

House by the Railroad, 1925—with its stark, dramatic composition—heralded the arrival of Hopper's artistic maturity, and his style changed little from then on. Subjects such as solitude, sailing and small-town life, which had been with him

Hopper (opposite page) forged his early style in Paris, where he painted *Le Pont des Arts* (above), and achieved his break- through in New York, when he sold *The Mansard Roof* (right) to the Brooklyn Museum in 1923.

since childhood, occupied him into his last years.

More than anything, though, Hopper's work was a personal treatise on the human condition, with loneliness, according to most critics and observers, as the central theme. Even characters who are not alone, as in *Nighthawks*, 1942, appear isolated, destined to spend long late-night hours sitting silently at a nondescript counter, locked in by the

precise geometry and harsh light of the diner. Hopper himself thought "the loneliness thing [was] overdone," that solitude might be a better word, though looking at the woman in *Automat*, 1927, with the electric light stark above her and the foreboding night looming at her back, it is hard not to read some pathos into her predicament.

Whether expressing solitude, loneliness, boredom or some other state of being, Hopper's human subjects are more reflections of the place they inhabit than actors upon it—a subtlety perfectly in keeping with Hopper's seeming fatalism. Indeed, Hopper could impart a feeling of inevitability without even using a human figure, as in *Lighthouse Hill*, 1927, a work in which he characteristically uses bold shadow and light to animate solid forms.

Hopper's lifelong examination of light, composition and geometry was informed no doubt by his love of theater and architecture. Formalistic concerns, however, were always secondary to his belief in art as an expression of self, a philosophy learned from his most influential teacher, Robert Henri, the leader of the so-called Ash Can Artists. As Hopper wrote in 1935, "The nucleus around which the artist's intellect builds his work is himself, the central ego, personality, or whatever it may be called, and this changes little from birth to death." Indeed, while other artists moved further into abstraction as the decades passed, Hopper never abandoned American realism. His *oeuvre* is one of the most consistent and uncompromised in modern American art.

Bold light and shadow animate *Lighthouse Hill* (opposite page), and a solitary figure looms in *House at Dusk* (above); in *Automat* (below), Hopper's theme of human isolation is apparent.

Aftermath

Hopper died peacefully in his New York City home on May 15, 1967, at 85. His use of formal elements to connect emotionally with viewers has become a standard for judging other artists. His influence was keenly felt in the 1960s and '70s—Hopper's use of commercial symbols, for example, presaged Andy Warhol's *Soup Cans.* Hopper's *House by the Railroad* has been credited with inspiring Norman Bates' hilltop dwelling in Hitchcock's 1960 thriller *Psycho*, and the spooky mansion of the Charles Addams cartoon family.

THE FOUR HORSEMEN

It is no coincidence that the 1920s, the decade we now hail as the Golden Age of American sports, was also the Golden Age of American sportswriting: Why perform miracles if no one's there to record them? Even heroes need press agents.

In that regard, the athletic gods of the 1920s—Babe Ruth, Jack Dempsey, Red Grange, Bobby Jones, and Bill Tilden—were fortunate indeed. There was a wealth of great sportswriters prepared to commemorate their feats, among them Westbrook Pegler, Ring Lardner and, most famous of all, Grantland Rice, who did not hesitate to use the classical education he had acquired at Vanderbilt to bathe his sweaty subjects in a golden light.

Four Horsemen of Notre Dame

Thus, football's Grange was "a will o' the wisp built of steel" and Jones a "modern Merlin who waved his magic wand that drove par into the background and made perfect golf, as the human knows it, look crude and listless."

Today that sort of rhetoric would sound ridiculous, so completely have cynicism and irony replaced wonder and sincerity. But Rice was at heart a moralist, and he employed heroic rhetoric unselfconsciously. He saw athletic competitions as tests of character as well as brawn, a conviction that appealed mightily to a nation exhausted by war. Indeed, his most famous line, from a poem called "Alumnus Football," which Rice wrote for a Vanderbilt reunion, was not about sports as much as sportsmanship: "For when the One Great Scorer comes to mark your name, He writes—not that you won or lost—but how you played the Game."

One of Rice's close friends was yet another of the decade's great sports figures, Notre Dame football coach Knute Rockne, who was probably more responsible than anyone else for the game's tremendous leap in popularity. Some of Rockne's ideas seem strange, no matter how effective they

The Four Horsemen of Miller, Layden, Crowley and Stuhldreher (opposite page, l. to r.) flourished under Rockne (above).

proved to be. His "starters" were often his second stringers, whom he used as "shock absorbers" to blunt the opposing team's energy before sending his best players onto the field in the second quarter. He also developed the Notre Dame "shift," in which backs shifted position prior to the snap. And most famously, he was a master of the pep talk, making so many stirring speeches that he even gets credit for one he probably did not make, the "Win one for the Gipper" address immortalized by Pat O'Brien in the movie *Knute Rockne—All American*, which also starred Ronald Reagan as the Gipper. In the 13 years he coached the Fighting Irish before dying in a plane crash in 1931, Rockne was 105-12-5 for a winning percentage of .881, still the highest in college football.

The national champion Fighting Irish of 1924 were probably one of the best college teams ever. Led by quarterback Harry Stuhldreher, fullback Elmer Layden and halfbacks Jim Crowley and Don Miller, all of whom were later elected to the College Football Hall of Fame, Notre Dame went 10–0 that season, beating its 10 over-matched foes by a cumulative score of 285–54. The Irish beat Stanford 27–10 in the Rose Bowl, with Layden making two interceptions, scoring three touchdowns and averaging 48.5 yards per punt with a long of *80* yards.

Army gave the Irish their toughest game that season, succumbing 13–7 in New York City's Polo Grounds to the balanced Notre Dame attack. Miller rushed for 148 yards, Crowley for 102 and Layden 60. Rice's account of the game in the following day's *New York Herald Tribune* made it all the more memorable:

Outlined against a blue-gray October sky, the Four Horsemen rode again.

In dramatic lore they are known as Famine, Pestilence, Destruction and Death. These are only aliases. Their real names are Stuhldreher, Miller,

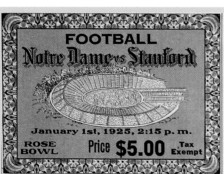

Led by the Four Horsemen (opposite page, below) and the running of Crowley (opposite, above), Notre Dame beat Army 13–7 (right) and capped its perfect season with a 27–10 triumph over Stanford in the Rose Bowl (above).

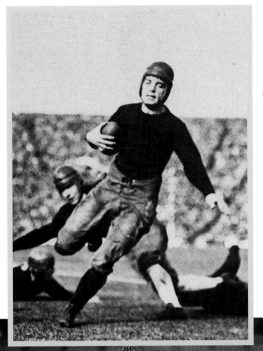

"Rockne was a bright, personable man. He was what the sportswriters today would call 'good copy.' He could be funny, caustic, controversial. Hardly a day went by when he wasn't quoted somewhere."

—*NOTRE DAME HALFBACK JIM CROWLEY*

The Four Horsemen

By Grantland Rice

POLO GROUNDS, N. Y., Oct. 18, 1924.—Outlined against a blue-gray October sky the Four Horsemen rode again.

In dramatic lore they are known as famine, pestilence, destruction and death. These are only aliases. Their real names are: Stuhldreher, Miller, Crowley and Layden. They formed the crest of the South Bend cyclone before which another fighting Army team was swept over the precipice at the Polo Grounds this afternoon as 55,000 spectators peered down upon the bewildering panorama spread out upon the green plain below.

A cyclone can't be snared. It may be surrounded but somewhere it breaks through to keep on going. When the cyclone starts from South Bend where the candle lights still gleam through the Indiana sycamores those in the way must take to the storm cellars at top speed. The cyclone struck again as Notre Dame beat the Army 13 to 7 with a set of backfield stars that ripped and rushed through a strong Army defense with more speed and power than the warring Cadets could meet.

Crowley and Layden. They formed the crest of the South Bend cyclone before which another fighting Army team was swept over the precipice at the Polo Grounds this afternoon as 55,000 spectators peered down on the bewildering panorama spread out upon the green plain below.

Rockne's student publicity aide, George Strickler, decided to translate Rice's prose into a photograph. Soon after the team returned to South Bend, he posed the four players, footballs tucked under their right arms, atop four horses, and gave the photo to the wire services, which spread it around the country.

"After that," joked the humble Miller, "we said a prayer for Granny almost every night because we knew we weren't that great. We have always felt that there were other backfields at Notre Dame superior to ours, such as the 1930 unit, but they never had a Grantland Rice for a press agent and we did."

The literary stylings of Rice (opposite page, above) did almost as much for the Notre Dame legend as the innovative Rockne (right and above, arms crossed) and the talented pool of players in his charge.

Aftermath

Rockne's winning legacy has continued, with Notre Dame producing a record seven Heisman Trophy winners: Angelo Bertelli (1943); John Lujack ('47); Leon Hart ('49); John Lattner ('53); Paul Hornung ('56); John Huarte ('64) and Tim Brown ('87). And, of course, Ronald Reagan—the Gipper himself—was elected president of the United States twice.

FLAPPERS

The world had never seen anything like her, and the world was not entirely pleased with what it saw. She drank too much, danced too much and flirted with total strangers. She wore skirts that were scandalously short and enjoyed evenings that were scandalously long. To the caustic social commentator H. L. Mencken, she was "a somewhat foolish girl, full of wild surmises and inclined to revolt against the precepts and admonitions of her elders."

She was the flapper—giggling, giddy, disturbing proof that the Victorian age of repressed sexuality was finally dead. She was somewhere between 16 and 30 years old, boyishly slim, and underneath the cloche perched so rakishly on her head, her hair was worn short, in the "bob" popularized by the actress Louise Brooks. Airhead though she sometimes was, the flapper soon came to represent the first significant youth culture in American history.

The flapper was portrayed most memorably in the fiction of F. Scott Fitzgerald, whose first short story collection was called *Flappers and Philosophers*, and the cartoons of John Held Jr., who arrived in New York City from Utah with $4 in his pocket but was soon earning $2,500 a week for the black-and-white drawings of flappers and their beaus that he made for magazines such as *The New Yorker* and *Life*. As Held's stylish drawings make clear, flapper fashion aimed for a long straight silhouette, with low waistlines, and hemlines so high they prompted the chief of police of tiny Sunbury, Pennsylvania, to issue an edict forbidding skirts that did not fall at least four inches below the knee. But that was surely an overreaction, for while the flapper perhaps revealed more of herself than her mother had, her look suggested androgyny more than promiscuity. Some flappers even bound their

In dizzying displays of silliness, the young did the Charleston (left) and exhausted themselves in dance marathons (above).

The Charleston had a famous proponent in Josephine Baker, who performed her own version in Paris (right); stylized images of the dance (below) appeared everywhere and as more and more took to the craze, couples labored to add new steps to the dance (opposite page).

"Not since 1820 has feminine apparel been so frankly abbreviated as at present; and never, on this side of the Atlantic, until you go back to the little summer frocks of Pocahontas."

—*BRUCE BLIVEN, writer, The New Republic, 1925*

breasts and starved themselves in pursuit of less curvaceous figures.

The shocking metamorphosis of young ladies into flappers in the 1920s was the result of many cultural factors. One was sheer relief that a horrifying war had come to an end. As Fitzgerald put it, "Something had to be done with all the nervous energy stored up and unexpended in the War." It was time for a party, and while the merriment often felt forced and hysterical, everyone in the smart set was desperate to be included.

The nation was flush. Money and booze were everywhere. Prohibition quickly proved to be a colossal miscalculation, turning many ordinary Americans overnight into mischievous kids hellbent on misbehaving. Sigmund Freud was on the tip of every tongue, and the sensual jazz of Louis Armstrong and Duke Ellington blared in speakeasies and open roadsters, which were also hastening the sexual revolution by providing young couples with havens far from their chaperones. As Cole Porter put it: "In olden days a glimpse of stocking/Was looked on as something shocking,/But now, God knows,/Anything goes."

The corollary to "anything goes" was that anything worth doing was worth doing to excess. Otherwise sane citizens sat atop flagpoles for days on end, and dance marathons were all the rage, some of them lasting months, far past the point at which the exhausted contestants had begun to hallucinate. A dance marathon in Chicago lasted 119 days!

The flapper's favorite dance was unquestion-

The fetching fashions (left) that became the rage revealed more of the female form, yet pushed toward androgyny (opposite page, below); though many were shocked by the displays of flesh, particularly at beaches (below), some of the older generation (opposite page, above) were not so scandalized.

revue *Runnin' Wild*. "Up on your heels, down on your toes" begin the dance's instructions, but what follows is not so easily described. With knees and toes turned in and heels flying up, dancers flapped their bent arms like chicken wings in time to the frenetic pace of the music.

The Charleston took Manhattan and then all of the nation by storm. By 1925 there supposedly were 400 moves to the dance. Less energetic dancers participated by crisscrossing their hands over their wobbling knees, as if shuffling them. Some considered the Charleston immoral, and it was banned on many college campuses. But to the flappers of the naughty, exuberant '20s, that was hardly a deterrent. If anything, it just added to the dance's allure.

ably the Charleston, and in that respect she was no different from most of her contemporaries. A manic, syncopated step done to fast 4/4 time, the Charleston probably originated among blacks in the South, either in South Carolina or New Orleans, and caused a sensation in 1923, when it made its stage debut in New York, in the all-black

Aftermath

The flappers' youthful rebellion challenged the status quo with new fashions, new attitudes and new behaviors. The next time a generation would so forcefully rock America would be in the 1960s, when young people again challenged the looks and lifestyles of an entire nation. The '60s, which took the skinny, androgynous look of the '20s even further in the person of fashion model Twiggy, were also kicked off with a distinctive dance, the Twist. For both generations, hard economic times brought the fun to a screeching halt.

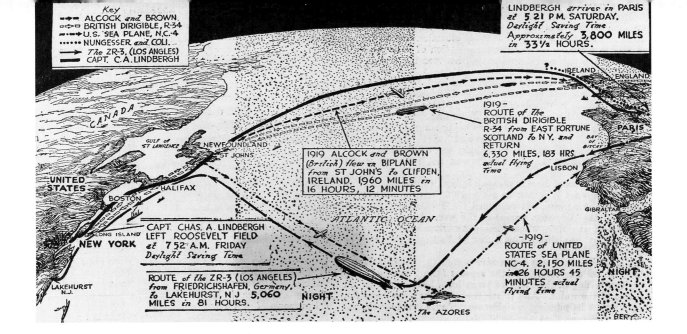

LINDBERGH arrives in PARIS at 5.21 P.M. SATURDAY, Daylight Saving Time. Approximately 3,800 MILES in 33½ HOURS.

1919 — ROUTE of the BRITISH DIRIGIBLE R-34 from EAST FORTUNE SCOTLAND to N.Y. and RETURN 6,330 MILES, 183 HRS. actual flying time

1919 ALCOCK and BROWN (British) flew in BIPLANE from ST JOHN'S to CLIFDEN, IRELAND, 1960 MILES in 16 HOURS, 12 MINUTES

CAPT. CHAS. A. LINDBERGH LEFT ROOSEVELT FIELD at 7.52 A.M. FRIDAY Daylight Saving Time

ROUTE of the ZR-3 (LOS ANGELES) from FRIEDRICHSHAFEN, Germany, to LAKEHURST, N J 5,060 MILES in 81 HOURS.

-1919- ROUTE of UNITED STATES SEA PLANE NC-4. 2,150 MILES in 26 HOURS 45 MINUTES actual flying time

CHARLES LINDBERGH

Flying alone over the Atlantic at altitudes as high as 10,000 feet in his single-engine plane the *Spirit of St. Louis*, Charles Lindbergh wondered if anyone was following his progress. Little did he know that upon reaching France he would be greeted by 100,000 delirious Parisians, who caused one of the largest traffic jams in their country's history. The seriousness with which the world was treating Lindbergh's flight was summed up by humorist Will Rogers, who wrote in his syndicated column: "No jokes today ... a slim, tall, bashful, smiling American boy is somewhere over the middle of the Atlantic Ocean where no lone human has ever ventured before...."

From the very beginning, the flight was fraught with danger. Departing from a muddy runway at New York's Roosevelt Field at 7:52 on the morning of May 20, 1927, Lindbergh's plane was barely able to maintain takeoff speed. It finally did lift off the ground with less than 100 yards of runway remaining. The plane lurched under the burden of the excess gasoline Lindbergh would need for his lengthy trip, and missed a stand of trees near the runway by a matter of yards. One Long Island reporter who witnessed Lindbergh's takeoff later likened his plane to a drunken sea gull. Lindbergh eventually stabilized the plane and flew over the misty Rhode Island shores on his way to Paris.

Over the Atlantic Lindbergh struggled to stay awake as his plane repeatedly dipped to within 10 feet of the turbulent waters. Blinded by heavy fog at one point, a surprised Lindbergh found himself flying directly into an ice storm. He adjusted his route before the plane's engines started to freeze over, narrowly escaping the perilous weather. It was 33 hours into, and very near the end of, his journey

Lindbergh's dramatic solo journey (top) transformed the modest aviator (left) into a media darling.

before Lindbergh was relaxed enough to bite into a sandwich.

At 10:00 p.m. on the second day of his flight the weary Lindbergh saw the welcoming lights of Paris in the distance. He touched down at Le Bourget airport at 10:21 p.m. on May 21 amidst hysterical acclaim and chaos. At that moment the "gangling teenager" entered the realm of myth. After stumbling from the cockpit, Lindbergh was hoisted up by the crowd while souvenir-seekers broke through barriers and ravaged his plane; police were needed to rescue both Lindbergh and his airplane from the eager hordes.

Lindbergh was born in 1902, the year before the Wright Brothers' first flight at Kitty Hawk. Ever independent, he dropped out of the University of Wisconsin during his sophomore year to pursue his abiding passion for aviation. Having learned the flight basics at the Nebraska Aircraft Corporation, Lindbergh became a barnstorming daredevil, performing death-defying stunts during which he would leave his co-pilot in the cockpit to walk out onto the lower wing while the plane swooped down near a group of stunned spectators. In other instances he would jump from the plane and fall freely for a few seconds before pulling the chord that opened his parachute.

In 1919, Franco-American philanthropist Raymond Orteig offered a $25,000 prize to the first person to fly solo across the Atlantic. By the time Lindbergh decided to take on the challenge eight years later, six men had died attempting the crossing. And Lindbergh had only five years of flight experience. More than a few observers considered

"[Lindbergh represents] the best traditions of the country…valiant in character, driven by an unconquerable will and inspired by the imagination and spirit of his Viking ancestors."

—PRESIDENT CALVIN COOLIDGE, 1927

After the *Spirit of St. Louis* (above) landed in France, police officials worked in vain to keep the crowds at bay (below); later Lindbergh acknowledged the screaming French crowds from the balcony of the U.S. Embassy in Paris (left).

his nickname, "The Flying Fool," entirely apt.

After his successful journey, Lindbergh was transformed in the public imagination; no longer "The Flying Fool," he would now forever be known as "Lucky Lindy" or the idealized "Lone Eagle." He returned to a hero's welcome in the United States, and was honored at the Capitol by one of the largest crowds in Washington history. In New York City, a massive ticker-tape parade greeted Lindbergh. Four-and-a-half million people lined the city sidewalks to catch a glimpse of the golden youth. Congress would later award Lindbergh the Medal of Honor, while partygoers honored him with a new dance step, the Lindy Hop.

Twenty-four years after the first flight at Kitty Hawk, Lindbergh had become the shining embodiment of human aspiration, a vivid symbol of the innovative, indomitable spirit of the era. In just over 33 hours "the slim, tall, bashful, smiling American boy" had made the world a much smaller place.

Lindbergh's flight produced banner headlines in *The New York Times* (above) as well as a ticker-tape parade in New York City (right) for the new American legend (top); Lindbergh and his wife, Anne Morrow (opposite page), who was also a pilot, later settled in England.

Aftermath

Charles Lindbergh was still a national hero when his 20-month-old son, Charles Jr., was kidnapped and then murdered in 1932. In what became known as the "Trial of the Century," Bruno Hauptmann was convicted and executed for the crime. Americans were riveted to the case, and soon after the trial, partly in order to escape the constant glare of publicity, Lindbergh left the country. Accompanied by his wife, Anne Morrow, and their second son, Jon, he moved to England. Positive prewar comments about Nazi Germany would tarnish Lindbergh's image in subsequent years, but no one could contest the impact he had on the progress of aviation. In 1997, 70 years after Lindbergh's historic flight, "The Lindbergh Project Team," a group of aeronautical engineers, researchers and educators, developed plans for a small plane, *The Atlantic Navigator*, to follow Lindbergh's route across the Atlantic. The plane will be flown by a computer and guided by modern navigation equipment. It is expected to become the first pilotless plane to cross the Atlantic.

VOTES for WOMEN
DR. SHAW
LONG
BRANCH CASINO
THURS. 26 8 P.M.

VOTES
FOR
WOMEN

VOTES for WOMEN
DR. SH
LONG
BRANCH CAS
THURS. AUG.

THE 19TH AMENDMENT

On August 26, 1920, when Tennessee narrowly became the 36th state to ratify the 19th Amendment to the Constitution, voting rights were at last extended to American women. Scores of suffragists who had sat knitting in the galleries of the nation's Capitol or standing in anticipation on its steps responded in a decidedly unladylike manner, "cheering," according to *The New York Times*, "like collegians after a football victory."

From the nation's inception, American women had been relegated to second-class status. Once married, in many states they were denied the right to own property, enter into contracts or sue their husbands for divorce. Married or not, women were prevented by law from voting. In the nineteenth century women began working to overturn these clearly discriminatory laws.

The seeds of the 19th Amendment were planted in July 1848 at a women's rights convention in Seneca Falls, New York. On the morning of July 19, Elizabeth Cady Stanton and Lucretia Mott unveiled a Declaration of Sentiments and 11 Resolutions, proposing that "woman is man's equal," and that she should "secure to [herself her] sacred right to elective franchise." Stanton and Mott were wives of abolitionists who had met at an anti-slavery convention eight years earlier. The fact that they were denied entrance to that convention's main hall because of their gender undoubtedly influenced their actions at Seneca Falls.

The movement unleashed in Seneca Falls recieved a giant push when Stanton met Susan B. Anthony at another anti-slavery gathering in 1851. A Quaker abolitionist and temperance worker, Anthony became a willing and able adherent to the suffragist cause. Her experiences organizing temperance societies fired her re-

The push for suffrage included local efforts (left) and a major rally in New York City, attended by 25,000 women (above).

Members of the National Woman's Party sold *The Suffragist* in Boston (opposite page), to keep women informed of the movement's progress; through the years suffragists pressed their case in Washington (right) and even in London (above).

Official Program WOMAN SUFFRAGE Procession

Washington D.C. March 3, 1913

formist drive: "As I passed from town to town," Anthony remembered, "I was made to feel the great evil of women's utter dependence on man.... Woman must have a purse of her own, and how can this be, so long as the law denies the wife that right?"

Stanton and Anthony formed a 50-year alliance in which, as Stanton once said, "I forged the thunderbolts and she fired them." Indeed, Anthony addressed every Congress between 1869 and 1906, speaking in support of women's rights.

At the end of the Civil War, a rift developed among feminists over whether to tie the cam-

paign for women's rights to the campaign to enfranchise former slaves. Stanton and Anthony argued strenuously for consitutional amendments that would give the right to vote to both groups. When the 15th Amendment, extending the vote to black men alone, was sent by Congress to the states for ratification, the duo split from Mott and others to form the National Woman Suffrage Association, which accepted only women and opposed the 15th Amendment for its failure to include women of any race.

"Mr. President, what will you do for woman suffrage? How long must women wait for liberty?"

—A plea to Woodrow Wilson on a banner carried by suffragists picketing the White House in 1913

Meanwhile, much of the public was debating not whether or not women should vote so much as what their proper role in society should be. In his rejection of women's suffrage, Senator Thomas Bayard of Delaware asked, "Under the operation of this amendment, what will become of the family hearthstone around which cluster the very best influences in human education?"

"Our ladies glow with a higher ambition," the *Philadelphia Public Ledger* wrote. "They soar to rule the hearts of their worshipers, and secure obedience by the spectre of affection...a woman is nobody. A wife is everything."

In such a climate, politicians were slow to respond to the suffragists' cries. William Howard Taft cautiously instructed them to collect more signatures on their petitions before he would take up their cause, and Theodore Roosevelt did not include women in his "progressive" campaign of 1912. Woodrow Wilson also dragged his feet. When he ran for reelec-

tion in 1916 on the slogan "He kept us out of war," suffragists retorted, "He kept us out of suffrage."

Anthony, whose death in 1906 prevented her from witnessing the success of her work, inspired her troops with this final public utterance: "Failure is impossible."

The suffragists lobbied on, receiving a needed boost during World War I, when the value of women in the war effort was well recognized. The 19th Amendment was introduced on January 20, 1918, by Jeanette Rankin, the first woman to be elected to Congress (she came from Montana, one of the first states in the country to grant women the right to vote). And by war's end it had cleared both houses of Congress and was sent on to the states for ratification. Soon the suffragists would have reason to cheer.

Aftermath

As women flocked to the polls in
greater numbers, they became a
political force to be reckoned
with. In years to come politicians
eager to woo women voters
would find it expedient to deal
with previously neglected issues
such as funding for child care,
workplace discrimination and
funding for public education. A
"gender gap" in the voting
habits of the electorate—
women are more likely to vote
Democratic, men Republican—
continues to cause heartburn for
political consultants across the
country. But the clearest indica-
tion of women's clout today is
the number of female elected officials; in 1997 there were 52
women in the U.S. House of Rep-
resentatives, nine in the Senate
and two serving as governors.

ELECTRIC TOY TRAINS

When the Carlisle and Finch Company of Cincinnati, Ohio, brought out America's first electric toy train—actually a brass streetcar—in 1896, the product was received as a scientific curiosity rather than a toy or a collector's item. Electricity itself was still something of a novelty, not yet a standard commodity in American households. Nevertheless, orders for the train outstripped the company's ability to supply them.

Four years later, in New York City, a promising young inventor named Joshua Lionel Cohen tinkered with a tiny electric motor in his office at 24 Murray Street. Just 23 years old, Cohen (who changed his surname to Cowen in 1910) had already invented a fuse for use in flash photography, as well as a prototype of the flashlight. He had begun his professional career at the tender age of 21, when he won a substantial contract with the navy to produce fuses for use in mines. Impressive as Cohen's previous accomplish-

ments were, his miniature motor truly was the start of something big. He founded the Lionel® Manufacturing Company in September 1900, and issued its first train, a wooden gondola car, the following year. Lionel®'s premier catalog, a 16-page black-and-white affair, appeared in 1902, and by 1917 the company employed 700 people.

Lionel®'s chief competitor in model railroading was the Ives toy company of Bridgeport, Connecticut. Founded in 1868 in Plymouth, Massachusetts, the company began producing clockwork, or windup, trains in 1901, and was among the first to put these on tracks. Ives trains took their designs from actual American locomotives, an idea that won many imitators. In 1910 Ives released its first electric train, and by the '20s the company dominated the U.S. market along with Lionel®.

Ives upped the ante in the competition between

Toy trains of every variety (left and above) became familiar household fixtures, particularly at Christmastime.

"Boys! See the lights flash on and off—see the gates go up and down—hear the warning bells ring! The Action is Automatic!"

—*LIONEL® TRAINS CATALOG, 1928*

the two companies in 1921, when it converted its largest line of trains from Gauge 1 to Standard Gauge. (Gauge refers to track width.) This move ultimately benefited both firms, because it broadened the market for Standard Gauge trains and accessories. The "classic period" of Standard Gauge equipment soon followed, as Ives and Lionel® added ever more intricate details and lifelike accouterments in attempts to top one another with each new line. The passenger sets Lionel® issued in the late '20s, including the State, Blue Comet and Stephen Girard sets, are coveted by hobbyists as the most beautiful model trains ever made.

Toy train sets became fixtures in American homes, and model railroading grew to be the

largest category in the U.S. toy industry. New products were trumpeted in the companies' colorful yearly catalogs, which became vital marketing tools and collectors' items in their own right.

As Lionel® and Ives gained momentum in the East, American Flyer came chugging out of the Midwest in 1907. Founded by the Edmunds-Metzel hardware company of Chicago, American Flyer introduced its first line of trains—clockwork models—in 1914. In 1918, American Flyer produced two million sets of windup locomotives. The company began manufacturing electric trains that year, and by 1926 was rolling along well enough to undertake a joint venture with Lionel® to buy the Ives company, which had been derailed by finan-

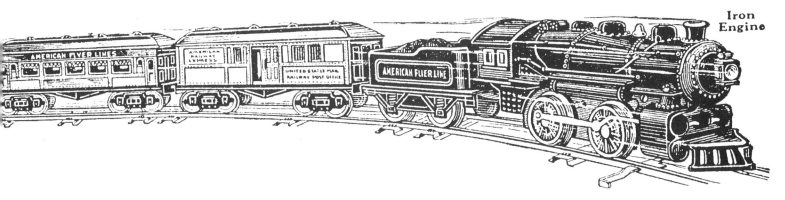

Iron
Engine

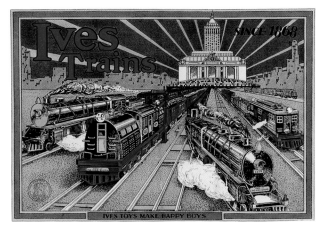

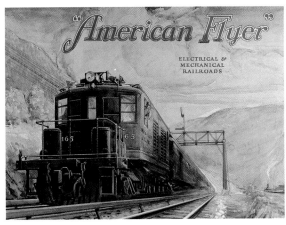

As increasing numbers of kids became train enthusiasts, the accompanying accouterments became more and more elaborate (opposite page); the early pioneers in toy train design were Lionel (above, left), Ives (above) and American Flyer (above, right).

cial woes. Lionel® soon bought out American Flyer's stake in the combined company, but the Chicago firm would remain an industry leader until 1965.

With the purchase of Ives, Lionel® now owned the patented "E-unit" feature, which allowed trains to reverse direction through a forerunner of remote control. The company went on to establish a long list of industry firsts, including automatic crossing gates, "Lockon" track connections, and real smoke emitting from its toy stacks, as it dominated the marketplace for close to four decades, into the late '50s. In 1927 Lionel® opened a showroom at 15 East 26th Street in New York City. With vast model railroad dioramas and product displays, the site was a popular tourist attraction for decades.

Aftermath

The Great Depression forced Lionel® founder J. L. Cowen to place the company into receivership in 1934. Ever resourceful, Cowen found his way out of the crisis later that year by marketing the Lionel® Disney Mickey & Minnie handcar. A windup toy priced at $1, it proved to be the ideal Depression-era item and helped reinvigorate the company.

Lionel'®s relationship with Disney endures to this day; the train company's diversification has increased to include a manufacturing pact with Samhongsa of South Korea and a research-and-development arm, Liontech, headed by rock musician Neil Young, a longtime toy train enthusiast.

In 1995, Wellspring Associates, a group of investors including Young, purchased Lionel®. The company will celebrate its 100th anniversary in 2000.

THE STOCK MARKET CRASH

"It has been 12 months of unprecedented advance, of wonderful prosperity," a *New York Times* editorial declared on New Year's Day 1929. "If there is any way of judging the future by the past, this new year will be one of felicitation and hopefulness."

While such unbridled optimism may seem laughably misguided in hindsight, the *Times* was by no means alone—or without reason—in its sanguine outlook. The industrial revolution had smiled upon the United States in the 1920s, sending the nation roaring out of a mild postwar recession and into its most promising economic era ever. Production and consumerism were up, as were corporate profits. In 1923, U.S. Steel was so far ahead of the game that it was able to reduce its workday from 12 to eight hours, hire 17,000 new employees and raise wages—and still show a profit at year's end. In 1926, 4,301,000 automobiles were produced in

Stock Market Crash 1929

the United States. Within three years that figure rose by more than a million, to 5,358,000. By comparison, in 1953, a bumper year for Detroit, 5,700,000 cars rolled off the assembly line. The leading pundits of the '20s could scarcely be faulted for failing to detect the devastating economic storm that was brewing.

With the economy growing by leaps and bounds, ordinary Americans began to invest in the stock market, long the province of the upper class. Investors developed a giddy faith in the possibility of getting rich quickly, and with minimal effort. They poured not only their discretionary income but also their savings and even borrowed money into the market. And the market reinforced investors' confidence, gaining in slow, steady increments for much of the '20s and displaying all the earmarks of reliability.

The boom gradually took on a momentum of its own, dangerously independent of the stocks'

The financial run produced by the crash on Wall Street (left) led thousands to sell whatever they could (above).

Police were needed to control the crowds (above and right) that gathered as the market plummeted, desperate for news of their financial plight; in the weeks that followed, unemployed workers resorted to selling apples to survive (opposite page).

actual value: The rising stock prices drew attention and buyers, which resulted in prices climbing still higher. "Expectations," John Kenneth Galbraith wrote in his 1954 classic, *The Great Crash*, "are thus justified by the very action that sends prices up." The market, in other words, was rising on a foundation no more solid than the (unfounded) optimism of its participants.

The first signs of trouble appeared in 1928, when stock prices began to shoot up. These gains were occasionally checked by precipitous losses, but the market would rebound even more strongly. Adding to the danger was the large amount of trading on margin. This phenomenon, which allowed investors to buy stocks with a down payment of as little as 10 percent—the remainder of the purchase price being financed by brokers' loans—added exponentially to the overblown market. In September 1929 the market peaked and then began its vertiginous descent. As prices plummeted, investors seeking capital for more margin sold off shares at desperation prices. According to one story, a woman who was presented by her broker with an astronomical bill for more margin cried out, "How could I lose $100,000? I never had $100,000." Hers was a common scenario, as brokers scrambling to pay off selling investors had to ask those who had bought on margin to cover the difference between their down payment and the actual purchase price. For this reason, the buy-

"Jerusalem has only one Wailing Wall; in Wall Street every wall is wet with tears."
—*ANONYMOUS,*
on Black Thursday

ing spree that had inflated the market was followed by a selling frenzy.

On October 24, Black Thursday, the market entered freefall, with the fevered exchange of nearly 13 million shares. J. P. Morgan & Company attempted a stopgap solution, sending Richard Whitney to the floor to buy $20 million in shares, which staved off disaster for exactly five days. The market collapsed altogether on October 29—Black Tuesday. More than 16 million shares changed hands that day, and $15 billion simply vanished. By mid-November that figure had reached $30 billion, and some four million people were out of work, more than three times the number of unemployed just one month earlier. The Roaring Twenties had indeed gone out with a bang.

Its financial heart wounded, the United States stumbled into the worst economic downturn in its history, the Great Depression. Factories, farms and banks closed en masse, and a vicious cycle of economic collapse took hold. In 1930, 1,300 banks failed; over the next two years 3,700 more closed their doors. People couldn't access their money, and therefore couldn't pump funds back into the economy. Despite President Herbert Hoover's insistence that prosperity was "just around the corner," the Depression would last more than a decade, eventually lifting with the help of the New Deal program instituted by President Franklin Delano Roosevelt in 1933.

The Depression produced some of the greatest hardships the nation has ever known, as soup lines (left) became commonplace and thousands of families like the one at right were forced to take to the road in search of work, often living in their cars or in one of the tent communities (below) that sprung up to serve transients.

Aftermath

Roosevelt was granted emergency powers to combat the Depression, and his New Deal mobilized an unprecedented federal relief effort. By 1940 the government had spent roughly $16 billion on direct relief and some $7 billion on public works.

The New Deal was not without its downsides—it rapidly increased the national debt, for one—but the overall effect was positive. America climbed slowly but surely out of its depression. Banks were closed, then reopened under tighter federal control. Business came under stricter regulation as well, and the era saw unprecedented redistribution of wealth. Labor gained new powers and the Social Security system was established. America would never suffer a collapse of such magnitude again.

INDEX

Aaron, Hank 23
Abbott, Robert 6
"Alumnus Football" 63
American Flyer 88, 89
American Museum of Natural History 17
American Realism 57
American Telephone and Telegraph Company (AT&T) 38
Amos 'n' Andy 39
Anthony, Susan B. 81, 82, 84
Armstrong, Louis 5, **6**, 7, **46**, 47, 48, 49, 50, 71
Art Deco 41, 42, 43, 44, 45
Ashcan Artists 60
Atlantic Navigator, The 79

Baker, Josephine **70**
Baldridge, Letitia 55
Baltimore Orioles 24
Basie, Count 51
Bateson, Gregory **17**, 18, 19, 20
Beiderbecke, Bix **49**, 50
Benny, Jack 39
Bertelli, Angelo 67
Black Thursday 93, 94
Black Tuesday 94
Bliven, Bruce 70
Bolden, Buddy 47
Boston Braves 27
Boston Red Sox 25, 26, 27
Bourget Field, Le 8, 75
Brooklyn Museum 57
Brooks, Louise 69
Brown, Tim 67
Burns, George 37

Calloway, Cab **50**
Canal Lock at Charenton **59**
Capone, Al 7, 14, 48
Charleston 5, **68**, 69, **70**, 72
Chicago Cubs 26
Chicago Defender 6
Chrysler Building **40**, 41, **42**, **43**
Chrysler, William 42
Cobb's Barns and Distant Houses **61**
Coming of Age in Samoa 18, 21
Constitutional Amendments
  15th Amendment 82
  18th Amendment 7, 11, 15
  19th Amendment 7, 81, 84, 85
Coolidge, Calvin 8, 15, 77
Cotton Club 47, **49**, 50
Cowen, Joshua Lionel 87, 89
Crosby, Bing 39
Crowley, Jim **62**, 63, 64, **65**

Daugherty, Harry 14
Dempsey, Jack 8, 63
Depression, the 9, 15, 44, 94, 95
Diamond, Jack (Legs) 47
Dorsey, Jimmy 50
Dorsey, Tommy 50
Dunn, Jack 24, 26
Dykes, Jimmy 23

"Echoes of the Jazz Age" 30
Eiffel Tower 42
Einstein, Izzy **13**
Eliot, T.S. 29, 30
Ellington, Duke 5, 7, 47, **48**, 49, 50, 51, 71
Emergency Quota Act 6
Empire State Building 43
Etiquette: The Blue Book of Social Usage 53, 54
Exposition Internationale des Arts Décoratifs et
  Industriels Modernes 41

Fall, Albert 8
Fitzgerald, F. Scott 5, 7, 9, **28**, 29, 30, 31, 32, 33, 69, 71
Fitzgerald, Scottie **28**, 29
Fitzgerald, Zelda **28**, 29, 32, 33
Flappers 5, **69**, 71, **72**, **73**
Flappers and Philosophers 69
Flight of the Moth, The 54

Foerstel, Lenora 20
Forbes Field 27
Ford, Henry 7
Four Horsemen, The **8**, **62**, 63, 64, **65**, 66, 67
Frazee, Harry 26
Freud, Sigmund 71

Galbraith, John Kenneth 92
Gates, Bill 32
Gatsby Style, 29, 30
Gershwin, George 7, 49, **51**
Goodrich, Lloyd 58, 60
Grange, Red 5, 8, 63
Great Crash, The 92
Great Gatsby, The 8, 29, 32
Growing Up In New Guinea 19

Harding, Warren G. 6, 8, 14, 35
Hart, Leon 67
Hauptmann, Bruno 79
Heisman Trophy 67
Held, John Jr. 69
Hemmingway, Ernest 29
Henderson, Fletcher 48, 50
Henri, Robert 60
Hitchcock, Alfred 61
Hoover, Herbert 9, 94
Hopper, Edward 57, **58**, 59, 60, 61
Hopper, Josephine Nivison 57
Hornung, Paul 67
House by the Railroad **56**, 57, 58, 61
Huarte, John 67
Huggins, Miller 23

Impressionism 57
Ives Company, The 87, 89

Jazz 7, 47, 48, 49, 50, 51
Jazz Age 5, 9, 29, 32
Jones, Bobby 8, 63

KDKA 35, 37
Key, Francis Scott 32
Kitty Hawk 76, 78
Knute Rockne—All American 64

Lardner, Ring 63
Lattner, John 67
Layden, Elmer **62**, 63, 64, **65**
League of Nations 5
Life 69
Lighthouse Hill 60, **61**
Lindbergh, Charles 5, 8, 38, **74**, 75, **76**, **77**, **78**, 79
Lindbergh, Charles Jr. 79
Lindbergh, Jon 79
Lionel Manufacturing Company 87, 88, 89
Lujack, John 67

Maloy, J.P. **34**, 35
Manhattan Bridge Loop **61**
Mansard Roof, The 58, 59
Marion Star 6
Maris, Roger 23
McCoy, Bill 13
Mead, Margaret **16**, **17**, 18, **19**, **20**, **21**
Mencken, H.L. 69
Miller, Don **62**, 63, 64, **65**, 66
Miss Manners 55
Moran, Bugsy 7
Morrow, Anne 78, **79**
Morton, Jelly Roll 7, 48, 50, **51**
Mott, Lucretia 81
Museum of Modern Art 58
Museum of Natural History 20

National Academy of Sciences 21
National Broadcasting Company (NBC) 38
National Origins Act 6
National Women's Christian Temperance Union 11
National Women's Party 82
National Woman Suffrage Association 82
New Deal, the 9, 94, 95
New Republic, The 70

New York City 7, 13, 44, 49, 50, 51, 72, 81, 89
New Yorker, The 69
New York Herald Tribune 64
New York Times, The **64**, **78**, 81
New York Yankees 23, 26, 27
Nighthawks **57**, 59

Oliver, Joe (King) 7, **47**, 48

Philadelphia Public Ledger 83
Polo Grounds 25, 64
Porter, Cole 71
Post, Edwin 54
Post, Elizabeth 55
Post, Emily **52**, **53**, **54**, **55**
Post, Peggy 55
Prohibition 7, 1, 13, 15, 71
Public Services Building (Portland) 45

Radio Corporation of America (RCA) 36, 38
Rankin, Jeanette 84
Reagan, Ronald 64, 67
Red Hot Peppers 50
Rhapsody in Blue 7
Rice, Grantland 63, **66**, 67
Rockne, Knute **8**, 63, 64, 65, **67**
Rogers, Will 75
Roosevelt Field 8, 75
Roosevelt, Franklin D. 15, 94, 95
Roosevelt, Theodore 83
Runnin' Wild 72
Ruth, Babe 4, 5, 8, **22**, **23**, **24**, **25**, **26**, **27**, 63

Sacco, Nicola 6
St. Mary's Industrial School for Boys 24
St. Valentine's Day Massacre 7, 39
Sarnoff, David 36
Seneca Falls, New York 81
Sex and Temperament in Three Primitive Societies 19
Smith, Bessie 7
Smith, Jess 14
Smith, Moe **13**
Speakeasies 13, **14**, 15
Spirit of St. Louis **8**, 75, **77**
Spock, Benjamin 19
Stanton, Elizabeth Cady 81, 82
Stein, Gertrude 28
Stuhldreher, Harry **62**, 63, 64, **65**
Sun Also Rises, The 29

Taft, William 11, 83
Tesla, Nicola 35
This Side of Paradise 31
Thorpe, Jim 26
Tilden, Bill 8, 93
Titanic 38
Twain, Mark 7
Twiggy 73
Twist, the 73

University of Notre Dame 8, 63, 64, 65, 66, 67

van Alen, William 42
Vanderbilt, Amy 55
Vanderbilt University 63
Vanzetti, Bartolomeo 6
Viennese Secession 41
Volstead Act 11, 14

Wall Street **90**, 91, 93
Waste Land, The 28
Westinghouse Electric 35
Whiteman, Paul 50, **51**
Wilson, Woodrow 5, 11, 83
World War I 5, 9, 84
World War II 44
World Series
  1924 35
  1932 23
Wright Brothers 76

Yankee Stadium 25, 27
Young, Neil 89

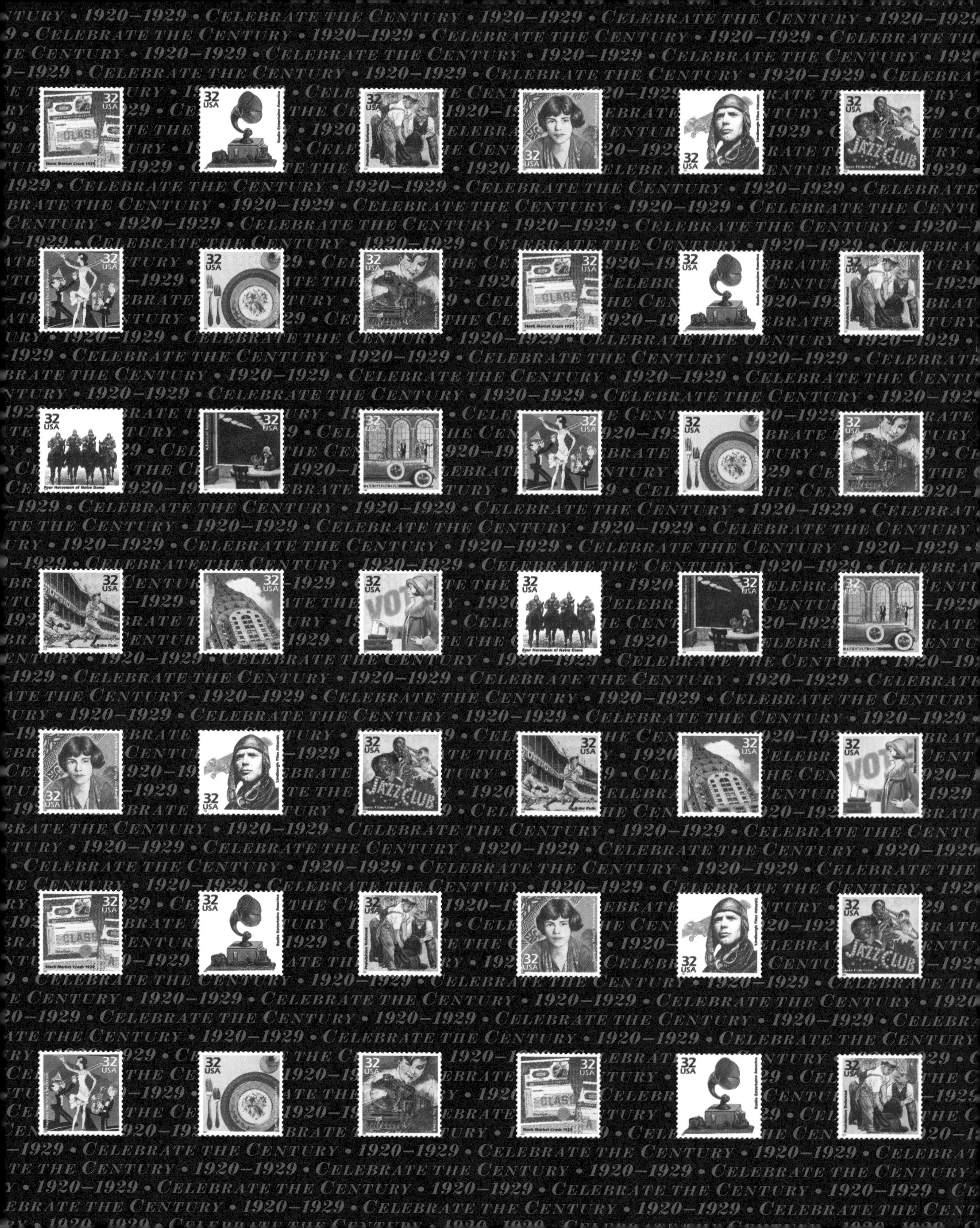
Celebrate the Century • 1920–1929